*Parables from
the Back
Side*

Parables from the Back Side

Bible Stories with a Twist

J. ELLSWORTH KALAS

Abingdon Press
NASHVILLE

PARABLES FROM THE BACK SIDE: BIBLE STORIES WITH A TWIST

Leader's Guide prepared by Shane Groth.

This book is printed on recycled, acid-free paper.

Library of Congress Cataloging-in-Publication Data

KALAS, J. ELLSWORTH, 1923–
    Parables from the back side : Bible stories with a twist / J. Ellsworth Kalas.
    p.   cm.
    Includes bibliographical references.
    ISBN 0-687-05697-7 (alk. paper)
    1. Jesus Christ—Parables—Sermons.   2. Methodist Church—Sermons.
    3. Sermons, American.   I. Title.
    BT375.2.K33   1991
    226.8'06—dc20   91-35952
                                                                                        CIP

Scripture quotations, except for brief paraphrases or unless otherwise noted, are from
the New Revised Standard Version Bible, copyright © 1989, or the Revised Standard
Version Bible, copyright 1946, 1952, 1971, by the Division of Christian Education of the
National Council of the Churches of Christ in the United States of America, and are
used by permission.

Scripture quotations noted NIV are taken from the *Holy Bible: New International
Version*. Copyright © 1973, 1978, 1984 by the International Bible Society. Used by permission of Zondervan Bible Publishers.

Those noted GNB are from the Good News Bible—Old Testament: Copyright ©
American Bible Society 1976; New Testament: Copyright © American Bible Society
1966, 1971, 1976.

Those noted KJV are from the King James or Authorized Version of the Bible.

00 01 02 03—20 19 18 17

MANUFACTURED IN THE UNITED STATES OF AMERICA

*To the memory of
Mother and Dad,
to acknowledge my debt
to their simple, earnest faith
in Christ*

I first read through the Bible, from Genesis 1 to Revelation 22, as an eleven-year-old. That same year I also preached what I perceived to be my first sermon, though those who invited me thought of it as a brief personal devotion.

Since then, more than half a century of Bible reading has gone by, and many thousands of sermons, yet still I marvel each day at the new light which breaks forth from the Book, and the excitement I feel in trying to preach and teach it with new insight. This book, *Parables from the Back Side*, is another expression of this lifelong experience.

I am grateful to members of the Abingdon editorial staff who have worked with me. They have eliminated so many instances of awkwardness or wordiness, yet without changing my thought or my personal style.

J. Ellsworth Kalas

CONTENTS

INTRODUCTION

*F*amiliarity doesn't always breed contempt, as the saying puts it, but it often breeds something potentially worse, the glazed eye. We quote favorite sayings and truisms so easily that we don't really hear them. In reading we may even underline or highlight them, not because they impress us but because they are familiar, and by our highlighting we pay them that most dubious of compliments, the passing nod so casual that we say a moment later, "Who was that I greeted?"

The parables of Jesus are in danger of such treatment. We've read them so often, have heard them taught or preached or have so expounded them ourselves, that their majestic brilliance hardly fazes us.

In this book I attempt to release some of the brilliance anew simply by turning the parable around and entering it from another side. I don't mean to detract from the basic teaching of the parable; rather, I hope to make such teaching more clear and biting.

P. G. Wodehouse, the British humorist, has one of his characters refer to a parable of Jesus' as looking like a "straightforward yarn when you begin to read it," but then you find that it has "something up its sleeve that pops out at you and leaves you flat."

That's my aim in approaching these beloved and perhaps too familiar stories from the back side. I'd like for them again to pop out at us and leave us, perhaps not flat, but examining our souls.

CHAPTER 1

When the Good Samaritan Is Bad News

LUKE 10:25-37: Just then a lawyer stood up to test Jesus. "Teacher," he said, "what must I do to inherit eternal life?" He said to him, "What is written in the law? What do you read there?" He answered, "You shall love the Lord your God with all your heart, and with all your soul, and with all your strength, and with all your mind; and your neighbor as yourself." And he said to him, "You have given the right answer; do this, and you will live."

But wanting to justify himself, he asked Jesus, "And who is my neighbor?" Jesus replied, "A man was going down from Jerusalem to Jericho, and fell into the hands of robbers, who stripped him, beat him, and went away, leaving him half dead. Now by chance a priest was going down that road; and when he saw him, he passed by on the other side. So likewise a Levite, when he came to the place and saw him, passed by on the other side. But a Samaritan while traveling came near him; and when he saw him, he was moved with pity. He went to him and bandaged his wounds, having poured oil and wine on them. Then he put him on his own animal, brought him to an inn, and took care of him. The next day he took out two denarii, gave them to the innkeeper, and said, 'Take care of him; and when I come back, I will repay you whatever more you spend.' Which of these three, do you think, was a neighbor to the man who fell into the hands of the robbers?" He said, "The one who showed him mercy." Jesus said to him, "Go and do likewise."

T he parables of Jesus are so much a part of our culture that people often refer to them without realizing they're talking religion. Take the phrase "the good Samaritan." You'll find it today in most large dictionaries, because it's part of our common speech. Probably everyone knows what you mean if you speak of someone being a "good Samaritan," even though they may have no idea that the term has its origins in a story Jesus told.

Like most of Jesus' parables, this story was born in the give-and-take of discussion. A lawyer asked Jesus what must he do to inherit eternal life. A lawyer in first-century Israel was really a theologian, because the law of the Jewish people was that section of their scriptures they referred to as the Books of Moses—the first five books of the Old Testament. To know the law, therefore, was to know the purpose and teachings of the Hebrew scriptures. One obeyed the law to please God, not to stay out of the courts.

Jesus answered the lawyer's question by noting that the greatest commandment actually has two parts: Love God with all your heart, soul, mind, and strength; and love your neighbor as yourself.

The lawyer saw the rightness of Jesus' answer, but he wanted a way out. Perhaps, like many of us, he wanted the law to be cut down to manageable size, and he knew the key to doing so was to limit the definition of neighbor. We can love some people without too much effort, so it would be convenient if the commandment were to apply only to such persons. "But who is my neighbor?" the lawyer asked.

So Jesus told the story of a man who was traveling home from Jerusalem to Jericho. Along the way, robbers attacked him, stripped him and beat him, then left him at the roadside, half dead. Soon, Jesus said, a priest came by. When he saw the man's condition, he steered his beast to the other side of the road and continued on his way. A little later another religious leader came by. He followed the same pattern.

Then a Samaritan came by. Jesus was speaking to a predominantly Jewish audience, and he knew full well how they felt about Samaritans. There was bad feeling among Jews and Samaritans that stretched back several hundred years. Jews despised Samaritans for both ethnic and religious reasons; they would go miles out of their way to avoid contact with them. And, of course, Samaritans felt much the same about Jews.

Now this Samaritan was clearly a very good human being. When he saw the battered, dying man, he put him on his donkey, took him to the nearest inn, nursed him through the night, and made provision for his care for as long as might be necessary. No wonder the term "good Samaritan" has found a place in our common speech!

It's easy to see the point of Jesus' story. I'm sure the lawyer saw it and was pained by it. Jesus wants us to realize the responsibility we have to our fellow human beings, and he wants us to understand that we are neighbors to the whole human race. It doesn't matter whether we know the other person, or whether his race or style of life is like our own; it doesn't even matter whether the person appeals to us or repulses us. Because someone is human and inhabits this planet with us, he or she is our neighbor. That's the point of the story.

Now let me approach the story from the back side. We usually focus our attention on the Samaritan or on the two religious leaders who preceded him. But what about the man who was robbed, beaten, and left to die? What shall we say about this man who was victimized by the robbers, ignored by the priest and the Levite, and then helped by a despised Samaritan? How did he feel about being helped by a Samaritan?

Jesus doesn't tell us that the victim was a Jew, but there's no doubt about it; it's an implied factor in the story. A Jew in trouble was ignored by his fellow Jews—who most easily filled the definition of "neighbor"—and then was helped by a Samaritan. How did this Jew feel about the experience?

We need to remember that we're talking about someone who had never associated with a Samaritan, not even in passing encounters. Perhaps he had never even spoken to one. Furthermore, he hoped it would always remain that way. But now, in his hour of deepest need, at a moment of life and death, it is a Samaritan who cleans his wounds, dresses them with oil and wine, binds the hurt places, lifts him to his donkey (perhaps panting with the effort), and carefully escorts him along the rugged road. At times the Samaritan speaks comfortingly. All night long he sleeps on the floor next to the injured man, attentive to any expression of pain or restlessness. I can imagine the Jew overhearing the Samaritan the next morning as he makes financial arrangements for the man's continued care.

How do you think the victim felt about all of this? That's easy, you answer; he was just glad to be alive. Not necessarily. There have been times when I, as a pastoral counselor, have suggested that a person seek help from a particular source or discuss his or her predicament with an employer or family member, only to hear the person answer, quickly and vigorously, "I'd rather die!" I don't think it is meant literally, but it is a graphic way of describing the intensity of the feelings involved.

So how do you think the Jewish victim felt when he realized he was getting all this help from a Samaritan? I wonder if he whispered to God, "It's good of you to send me help. But couldn't you have sent a nice Jewish man? Why this Samaritan?"

One bright October day several years ago I was hurrying to downtown Cleveland, Ohio, for a luncheon appointment with a businessman in my congregation. I had been delayed at the last minute by a phone call, as often is the case, so I was hurrying. Hurrying so much, in fact, that I gambled on my fuel supply.

Suddenly, in a rather disreputable section of downtown, my car sputtered and died. I eased out of the main lane of traffic while other cars hurried by; some of the drivers frowned at the delay. As I got out of the car, I noticed two men across the street standing in front of one of the "girlie shows" that dotted the area. They quickly hurried across the busy street to ask if they might help me.

I explained that the problem wasn't engine trouble but just my stupidity in trying to travel without an adequate supply of fuel. I inquired about the nearest service station. They immediately answered with an easier solution. "I'll siphon some gas out of my tank," one man said, "and I'll pour it into yours. It'll be enough to get you to a filling station." I argued against the plan; I'd siphoned gas a few times as a teenager, so I knew what an unpleasant experience it can be. But the two men were insistent.

I talked with one man while his friend got a container and a hose, dropped to his knees beside his car, and sucked away at the hose until, at last, he put the gas-filled hose into his container as he spat out the portion he'd taken into his mouth. They then poured the gasoline into my carburetor and tank, and soon my motor was humming.

I tried to pay them. "Not on your life," they said. "We were just going for a late breakfast and we had time on our hands." "Let me buy your breakfasts," I pleaded, holding out a bill. But by this time they were already walking away from me, full of good humor. "Wouldn't think of it," one of them said. "This is just the sort of thing one fellow ought to do for another."

As I drove on my way, pondering how much the two men had done for me and how cheerfully they'd done it, I reviewed the conversation I'd had with the one man while his companion was getting the gasoline for my car. Making small talk, I had asked what he and his friend did for a living.

"We work for this fellow who runs girlie shows," he'd answered. "He buys a building and we fix it up for him and then we run it. He gets a few pretty girls, you know, who put on about three shows a night. They take off all their clothes and dance around naked, while we shine colored lights on them. It's a pretty good business. Lots of men come."

I'm a fairly open-minded fellow. When I was a teenager I delivered laundry in rundown houses of prostitution, gambling dens, and places where they examined me through a peephole before unbarring several locks to let me in. I've learned to understand many offbeat life-styles. I think I have patience with almost every sin except self-righteousness and pomposity. But this was the day I began sympathizing with the man the good Samaritan helped. I said to the Lord, "How come the person who stopped to help me wasn't someone with a bumper sticker that read, 'Honk if you love Jesus'? Or maybe one of my friends who was driving downtown to attend a board meeting for the United Way or the YMCA? Why did my good Samaritan have to be two fellows who run a girlie show?"

And that, I can't help feeling, is the sort of question that was in the mind of the Jew who had been beaten and left to die.

I'm sure God has a warm and gentle sense of humor. He so often sends blessings into our lives through unlikely channels. Let me warn you: As surely as you harbor ill feelings against some ethnic, racial, or intellectual group, or some particular class of people, you can expect that someday, somehow God will allow such a person to touch your life in some strange and helpful way. The good Samaritan so often is bad news to our preferences and prejudices.

Liz Burns had to learn that. She was a New York socialite who was accustomed to the privilege and protection of her position. Her divorce was front-page news, because it was the first million-dollar settlement. She was also terribly lost—alcoholic, psychotic, and bedeviled. Then she met Christ and was wondrously transformed. But she knew that she needed spiritual guidance, so she set out to find a minister through the help of a Christian neighbor.

Whom did God send her way? His clothes, Liz said, were shabby

and unpressed, and they hung loosely on his gaunt frame. He wore
farm shoes that were laced over and back on metal hooks. When he
sat down, Liz noticed that hanging from one green-black sock was
what looked like a piece of broken garter. "This," she recalled later,
"was the Reverend Gordon Rogers, man of God."[1] And he was just
what she needed, though he wasn't what she might have ordered.
God knew she needed a good Samaritan, and that's what he sent
her.

You and I have good reason to understand the story, because of the
way our salvation has come to us. You see, we are walking down a
road as perilous as the journey from Jerusalem to Jericho, the journey
we make from birth to death. It is a road of exquisite beauty and
adventure, but also one of great peril. So great, in fact, that we cannot
make the journey without being beset, from time to time, by thieves
and ruffians. You know some of their names: despair, unremitting
loneliness, unreasoning fear, lust, anger, crushing defeat. Whatever
the name, they are part of the kingdom of sin. They spring upon us
when we are least ready, and eventually they beat us and leave us half
dead—yes, and worse; for their attack is such that, unless help
comes, we surely will die.

Lying in that half-dead state, unable to help ourselves, we hear
footsteps approaching. We recognize the traveler as one whose help
we welcome, for he will let us pay our own way, so we can hold on to
our self-regard. We explain that we are deserving, that our
credentials are good, that we've always had a good record. But the
stranger passes us by. He is able to help only those who don't need
help, and, at best, his help is superficial and temporary. In truth, no
one can pay his or her own way in our predicament; after all, we've
been robbed and stripped, so how can we pay our way?

Now another stranger appears. We appeal to him on the basis of
our sincerity. We never intended to get into trouble, and the
circumstances aren't really our fault. We've meant well; doesn't
sincerity count for anything? But as the stranger passes, we realize
that of itself, sincerity is no virtue. After all, it's possible to be
sincerely wrong. And, sincere or not, we're in trouble.

Then a third Stranger comes. Clearly, he is a Samaritan, for he
carries a cross, and we remember that the ancient scripture says,
"Cursed is anyone who hangs on a tree."[2] Still worse, as he draws
near, we remember a description from long ago:

He was despised and rejected . . .
a man of sorrows, and acquainted with grief;
. . . .
he was despised, and we esteemed him not.[3]

A Samaritan, indeed!

But he volunteers to help. We try to explain: "I can pay my own way. I'm a deserving person, you know." The Stranger answers, "No one can purchase what I offer, nor can anyone deserve it. But I shall be glad to give it to you." And he lifts us to his donkey, a wondrously awkward beast called Grace.

But you and I don't want that kind of help. This Samaritan embarrasses us by his very kindness and mercy, because he won't let us pay our way, and because he isn't impressed by our credentials. It is a gift that we can never, in any way, repay. Sometimes we think we'd rather die in our lostness than humble ourselves to receive this Stranger's gift.

I have a feeling that the dying man in Jesus' parable must have felt that way when his help came by way of a despised Samaritan, and I know full well that you and I draw back when God's Eternal Samaritan extends his offer. We accept him only when our need is so desperate that we must accept him; only when we confess that we are powerless to help ourselves; and only when we see what love this Divine Samaritan offers.

Only then are we willing to be lifted onto the donkey called Grace and ride it, alongside Christ the Samaritan, into God's safe and eternal lodging.

CHAPTER 2

God Called a Party, but Nobody Came

LUKE 15:1-24: Now all the tax collectors and sinners were coming near to listen to him. And the Pharisees and the scribes were grumbling and saying, "This fellow welcomes sinners and eats with them."

So he told them this parable: "Which one of you, having a hundred sheep and losing one of them, does not leave the ninety-nine in the wilderness and go after the one that is lost until he finds it? When he has found it, he lays it on his shoulders and rejoices. And when he comes home, he calls together his friends and neighbors, saying to them, 'Rejoice with me, for I have found my sheep that was lost.' Just so, I tell you, there will be more joy in heaven over one sinner who repents than over ninety-nine righteous persons who need no repentance.

"Or what woman having ten silver coins, if she loses one of them, does not light a lamp, sweep the house, and search carefully until she finds it? When she has found it, she calls together her friends and neighbors,

saying, 'Rejoice with me, for I have found the coin that I had lost.' Just so, I tell you, there is joy in the presence of the angels of God over one sinner who repents."

Then Jesus said, "There was a man who had two sons. The younger of them said to his father, 'Father, give me the share of the property that will belong to me.' So he divided his property between them. A few days later the younger son gathered all he had and traveled to a distant country, and there he squandered his property in dissolute living. When he had spent everything, a severe famine took place throughout that country, and he began to be in need. So he went and hired himself out to one of the citizens of that country, who sent him to his fields to feed pigs. He would gladly have filled himself with the pods that the pigs were eating; and no one gave him anything. But when he came to himself he said, 'How many of my father's hired hands have bread enough and to spare, but here I am dying of hunger! I will get up and go to my father, and I will say to him, "Father, I have sinned against heaven and before you; I am no longer worthy to be called your son; treat me like one of your hired hands."' So he set off and went to his father. But while he was still far off, his father saw him and was filled with compassion; he ran and put his arms around him and kissed him. Then the son said to him, 'Father, I have sinned against heaven and before you; I am no longer worthy to be called your son.' But the father said to his slaves, 'Quickly, bring out a robe—the best one—and put it on him; put a ring on his finger and sandals on his feet. And get the fatted calf and kill it, and let us eat and celebrate; for this son of mine was dead and is alive again; he was lost and is found!' And they began to celebrate.

God is a party-giver. Some people in Jesus' day didn't understand that. In fact, it had never occurred to them, so when Jesus announced it—and *lived* it—they were at first confused, then troubled, and at last angered.

They had their own idea of what God is like. They saw God as an object of religious devotion and as the giver of the Law; and, to a degree, their understanding was right. But most of them had lost the feeling for the commandments characterized by the psalmist when he sang, "How love I thy law!" Instead, they had come to see the Law as a set of painful restrictions which not only must be obeyed but also carefully scrutinized to determine if the restrictions could be made even more exact and demanding.

No wonder many of these people became upset with Jesus. They could see that he was a good person and that he had all the marks of a true prophet of God, but, to their distress, he didn't choose to associate primarily with people like themselves. For reasons they couldn't understand, he spent most of his time with men and women whom they classified as sinners.

It's hard to know just how bad these sinners were. Some, like the tax collectors, were patently dishonest and were traitors to their own people. Others were women of the street. But most of the group that laid the strongest claim to Jesus were run-of-the-mill sinners: people who didn't fulfill the rather intricate requirements of the Jewish ceremonial and religious law, particularly as the meticulously religious interpreted it.

The Pharisees and scribes, who were considered the best people around (especially in their own eyes), wouldn't have anything to do with such people. These people were forbidden to eat in their homes or to be their guests. As much as possible, they even avoided doing business with them. Basically, as William Barclay has pointed out, the scribes and Pharisees didn't really want such persons to be converted; they would rather they be destroyed. They despised them for their failure to fulfill the Law as they interpreted it, they wanted nothing to do with them, and they wished that they would disappear from the face of the earth.

So it puzzled the scribes and Pharisees that Jesus spent time with such people. Worse yet, he even seemed to enjoy their company! One day they expressed these sentiments loudly enough that Jesus overheard them: "This man welcomes sinners and eats with them."

It was under these circumstances that Jesus told the people— especially the religious leaders—three stories. These stories constitute what may well be the most beautiful chapter in all of the Bible, a chapter evangelist Uldine Utley used to call "God's Lost and Found Department."

Jesus began the series of stories in a very personal way. "Which one of you," he asked, pointing an inquiring finger at those in the circle of listeners, "if he has a hundred sheep and loses one of them, doesn't go out to look for that lost one? And when he finds it, he's happy. He wraps the little thing around his shoulders and carries it home. Then he calls together his friends and neighbors. 'Celebrate with me,' he says, 'because I've found the sheep that was lost.'"

Everyone in the crowd recognized the scene. The men, especially, listened attentively. They had known times like that. In a little village, where two or three shepherds cared for the sheep which belonged to everyone in town, people sometimes waited long into the night for a shepherd to return, hoping and praying the lost sheep had been found. They wouldn't necessarily know if it was their sheep or their neighbor's, but the sense of community was so strong that the pain of loss was equally shared. If the shepherd returned with the lost sheep, the huddled, worried crowd would burst into cheers and tears of joy.

Now Jesus directed his attention to the women. "Suppose," he said, "a woman had ten silver pieces, and lost one." All the women (and the men, too, for that matter) knew that this was a serious loss. A silver piece represented roughly a day's wages in that first-century world, where most people survived from one day to the next. Jesus also might have had in mind the headdress that married women wore. These bands were made up of ten silver coins, held together by a silver chain. Girls sometimes saved for years to collect their ten coins. To lose one was almost like losing your feminine honor.

Whether the lost coin in Jesus' parable was treasured for its intrinsic worth or for its sentimental value, we don't know. We know only that when the woman lost it, she became frantic. For her, it was a tragedy. Her little house was dark, since it received light only through one small circular window. To find a tiny coin was nearly impossible, because the floor was nothing other than beaten earth covered with dried reeds and rushes. How could a person find a coin in such a place? Well, Jesus said that she lighted a lamp and swept the house. I expect she prayed every moment; with each swish of the broom, she must have strained to spot the tiny coin.

Then she found it! She quickly called together friends and neighbors. "Let's have a celebration!" she cried. "I've found the silver piece I lost!" The women in the crowd, and a few men, too, nodded with understanding. They could see why there'd be a great celebration.

Then Jesus told a story of a father with two sons. The younger of them left home. After he had squandered his inheritance, he came back—ashamed, beaten by experience, half-starved. But he looked beautiful to his father. The father had thought he was dead, so this emaciated, pathetic creature was glorious to behold. "We're going to have a party!" the father shouted. "Get the orchestra, tell the cook to do his utmost, spread the good news! My boy is alive, and he's come home!"

As you can see, these three stories follow the same plot line: Act One, something valuable is lost; Act Two, the lost is found; Act Three, they have a party! Jesus was very clear about the point of the stories. He concluded the stories of the sheep and the coin with virtually the same refrain: "Just so, I tell you, there is joy before the angels of God over one sinner who repents."[1]

When we read these three stories, we're usually inclined to concentrate on the sheep, the coin, and the wandering son. We don't give much thought, unfortunately, to the people Jesus had in mind, those critics who wondered why he associated with sinners—the people Jesus symbolized in the personality of the elder brother. But I'd like to turn the light of this story on God. These three parables conclude with the fact that God has a problem. And it makes me feel sorry for God.

I wonder if a light dawned on Jesus' religious listeners as he finished the three stories. More important, does a light dawn on us religious folk today? If the scribes and Pharisees were sensitive to what Jesus was saying, they probably drew two conclusions.

First, if the return of a sinner causes *heaven* to celebrate, as Jesus said three times, then such a return must be a profoundly important event. That probably shocked the religious community, provided they got the point, for they found sinners distasteful. Yet the angels in heaven thought it a matter of supreme joy that sinners would come home to God.

The second conclusion was probably even more difficult to reach; so much so that I'm not sure the people came to it at all. Jesus said that when the sheep, the coin, and the wandering son were found, the people called their friends and neighbors to celebrate. So it is, Jesus said, that when a sinner repents, the angels of heaven rejoice. They gave a party!

But now, the question: Where are God's friends and neighbors? Why does God have to depend on angels? Doesn't God have any friends?

Angels aren't the best ones to celebrate the return of sinners, because they don't have firsthand knowledge of sin and redemption. The thing that made the friends and neighbors such good party-goers in Jesus' stories is that they knew something about losing and finding, or about being lost and being found. They could throw their arms around the shepherd or the homemaker and say, "Do I ever know how you feel! I've had the same experience." But what do angels know about being lost and being found? These are experiences beyond the realm of their knowledge. A wonderfully sentimental revival song says that when we human beings sing redemption's story, the angels will "fold their wings," because they've never felt the joy of salvation. Angels really aren't the best party-goers.

So much of the joy of celebration comes in sharing it with others. Can you imagine how the shepherd and the homemaker would have felt if there had been no friends to rejoice with them? And how would you feel if your son or daughter had been gone for several years— perhaps missing in action—and then reappeared, wanting to come home. You'd have to tell someone, wouldn't you? If there were no friends in reach, you'd grab someone on the street corner, or you'd begin a conversation with a stranger on an airplane: "Do you know what? My son—he was lost. I thought he was dead. But he's alive! Say, could I take you out to dinner? I have to celebrate. Will you celebrate with me?"

That's why I feel sorry for God, and that's what Jesus wanted to get across to the scribes and the Pharisees—and perhaps to many of us church people today. God is divinely happy because some struggling sinner has come home; so he calls a party. Heaven sends an invitation to all those people who ought to be thrilled. God says to us religious people, "Come, celebrate with me! A poor fellow who was disreputable has just become a new man. And a woman who was indifferent to life and to heaven has become sensitive to me. They're both a little on the rough side, but they've been found. As a religious person, you'll be glad, and that's why I'm inviting you to celebrate with me."

But the sad news is that nobody comes—not many, at any rate; not enough. So I picture God saying to one of his archangels, "We'd better call the angels together to rejoice, this party won't amount to much." A knowledgeable angel hesitates and says, "We're not much good for a party like this, because we don't really understand salvation. What you need are some of those human beings, who know what it is to have been lost and now to be found."

"I know," God answers. "Those are the folks who should come. But for some reason or other, they don't want to. They don't seem to care about my party. They don't feel my joy."

The younger son in the third story must have been overjoyed at the party his father held in his honor. But just as certain, his joy must have been diminished when he learned that his older brother refused to take part in the celebration.

So it has been with many who have been found by Jesus Christ. Christopher Smart was one of the most brilliant poets in eighteenth-century England. Then his life fell apart. He went through a time of mental instability and heavy drinking until, at last, in a state of deep depression, he became a convinced and enthusiastic Christian. In fact, his earnestness for Christ brought him severe persecution in the years that followed. One of his finest poems contains this poignant line:

> For I am come home again, but there is nobody to kill the calf or to play the musick.[2]

How often do churches fail to kill a calf and play the music when a prodigal comes home? I'm afraid that sometimes there are people in the church who don't feel very glad that a soul has returned to God. Like the Pharisees of Jesus' day, they're skeptical of God's taste in bothering with such questionable persons. Or, they feel so uncomfortable with people of this sort that they wish they didn't come into the church.

In my boyhood, most churches had one or several converted alcoholics who had come to deliverance through new life in Christ. Today many churches have nearly ceded their outreach to alcoholics to Alcoholics Anonymous. Is it partly because the alcoholic finds a warmer welcome—a bigger party, if you please—in the AA meeting than in the church?

Several years ago a church of which I was pastor did a beautiful thing. Well over a hundred persons purchased Christmas presents for children in the ghetto and for children of convicts. I was so proud of the generous, loving response. Then I was troubled by a question: Suppose some of the welfare mothers had begun coming to our church, or suppose one of the convicts, just released from the state penitentiary, had come—how would my people respond? Would they work as hard to bring such persons into their adult Sunday school classes as they did when a bank president or a college professor joined? Would they ring the bells of heaven as happily for them as for the "good people" who appeared?

Perhaps some people in our churches don't even know how to rejoice. It may be that they've forgotten what it was like to be lost, so they can't understand the reason for a party. Or perhaps, like the older brother in Jesus' parable, they aren't sure that they, themselves, really belong to the family; so when they see a homecoming celebration, it makes them uneasy.

Poor, dear, loving God! There's nothing the divine Heart wants so much as to have the whole family come home, to have all the lost sheep, lost coins, and lost sons and daughters found. So each time someone is found, God says, "Let's have a party! Sally has won the victory over depression; Pete has dared to come to a church where everyone else has more money and better jobs; Mary has been delivered from alcoholism. It's time to celebrate!"

But God is short on friends. A great many people join churches and call themselves Christians, yet they can't get enthusiastic enough to join God's party. Heaven's joy makes them uneasy.

Meanwhile, a little group of God's "friends and neighbors" help the angels sing. They feel the gladness of God's dear heart, and they join in heaven's party.

CHAPTER 3

The Timid Soul

MATTHEW 25:14-30: "For it is as if a man, going on a journey, summoned his slaves and entrusted his property to them; to one he gave five talents, to another two, to another one, to each according to his ability. Then he went away. The one who had received the five talents went off at once and traded with them, and made five more talents. In the same way, the one who had the two talents made two more talents. But the one who had received the one talent went off and dug a hole in the ground and hid his master's money. After a long time the master of those slaves came and settled accounts with them. Then the one who had received the five talents came forward, bringing five more talents, saying, 'Master, you handed over to me five talents; see, I have made five more talents.' His master said to him, 'Well done, good and trustworthy slave; you have been trustworthy in a few things, I will put you in charge of many things; enter into the joy of your master.' And the one with the two talents also came forward, saying, 'Master, you handed over to me two talents; see, I have made two more talents.' His master said to him, 'Well done, good and trustworthy slave; you have been trustworthy in a few things, I will put you in charge of many things; enter into the joy of your master.' Then the one who had received the one talent also came forward, saying, 'Master, I knew that you were a harsh man, reaping where you did not sow, and gathering where you did not scatter seed; so I was afraid, and I went and hid your talent in the ground. Here you have what is yours.' But his master replied, 'You wicked and lazy slave! You knew, did you, that I reap where I did not sow, and gather where I did not scatter? Then you ought to have invested my money with the bankers, and on my return I would have received what was my own with interest. So take the talent from him, and give it to the one with the ten talents. For to all those who have, more will be given, and they will have an abundance; but from those who have nothing, even what they have will be taken away. As for this worthless slave, throw him into the outer darkness, where there will be weeping and gnashing of teeth.'"

*T*he people just ahead of me in the airport ticket line were discussing the National Football League play-offs. "I'm pulling for the Broncos," the woman said. "Why? Do you have personal ties to Denver?" asked the man standing beside her. "No. It's just that I'm always for the underdog," she replied.

Many of us are like that woman. For that reason we have trouble with one of the stories Jesus told. As a matter of fact, it's a story he must have told a number of times, because it appears in several different versions. Perhaps he revised it for different settings, to appeal in a special way to particular groups.

As Matthew records the story (25:14-30), a man of some substance was leaving for an extended journey. He reasoned that his interests would be best served if he put some of his resources in the direct control of some of his servants. He gave one of them five talents—let's say $5,000. Another, two, and a third, one.[1]

When he returned, the men came in for an accounting. The one who had received five talents reported proudly that he had doubled the investment; he now had ten talents. The man with two talents had been comparably successful; his store had increased to four talents. Both men were warmly praised by their employer. After all, that's the kind of person one wants in charge of one's business.

Then the underdog came in. He wasn't a brilliant person, particularly compared with his fellow workers. Worse yet, he lacked self-confidence. When he went out with his master's money, all he could think of was that his employer was a hard man, one who insisted on a good return from every investment. The world of business frightened him. Suppose he invested in a project and it failed? Or suppose he put the money in a bank and the bank collapsed? Suppose when his boss returned he could give him only $875 for the $1000 with which he had been entrusted?

It was all very frightening, and he was a timid man. He was the kind of man who, as some people would say, wore both a belt and suspenders. He did well enough under other people's direction, but he was terrified at the prospect of making decisions for himself—and all the more terrified when those decisions affected his employer's welfare. So he did the safe thing: He buried the money in the ground.

In a way, he was rather proud of himself. He was accustomed to being a loser, but in this case, he hadn't lost a thing. When his employer called him in for a report, he explained his course of reasoning and then said, "Here it is, sir. Every cent of it. Just as you entrusted it to me. Not a penny has been lost."

Frankly, my heart goes out to him. He's the slow-footed player who chooses to remain on first base when a faster player would try for second. He's the "C" student who decides to report on a "safe" subject when a better student would venture a tougher assignment. He may even be the person who works forty years for the same company while more daring neighbors move about. He's surely not a bad man. Timid, yes, but not bad.

But note how his employer treated him. "You wicked, lazy servant! So you know I'm a tough operator. Then why didn't you act accordingly?"

With that, the executive took the man's carefully hoarded sum, gave it to the person who already had ten talents, and commanded, "Throw that worthless servant outside, into the darkness, where there will be weeping and gnashing of teeth."[2]

Preacher and author Paul L. Moore recalls an old story about two farmers visiting over a fence in early spring. "Jake," the first said, "what are you going to plant this year, corn?"

"Nope, scared of the corn borer."

"What about potatoes?"

"Nope, too much danger of potato bugs."

The neighbor pressed on. "Well, then, what are you going to plant?"

Jake answered, "Nothing. I'm going to play it safe."[3]

Jake is an amusing figure, the community ne'er-do-well, a source of unending anecdotes. But there's nothing quaint or amusing about the timid soul in Jesus' parable. His story has no humor to relieve us; it has only tragedy.

Jesus is telling us what life is like. In this parable the loving Teacher is the no-nonsense, pragmatic rabbi who talks with us not on the basis of how we wish things were, but on the basis of how things are. Jesus is saying that what we don't use, we lose. It isn't a story of kindness or severity, but simply a report on how life works.

Nevertheless, I want to know more about this timid soul. What made him like this? Did he come from a long line of defeated people? In our nation's populace are pockets, in certain rural areas and in some city ghettos, where defeat is the order of life. No one expects to succeed, and no one expects anyone else to succeed. Was he that kind of person? Did he never have a teacher who inspired him to make the most of himself or a neighbor who talked with him about his potential?

As a boy, I read and reread dime editions of the novels of Horatio Alger, Jr., the great advocate of success. The titles were calls to achievement: *Strive and Succeed*, or *Onward and Upward*, for example. The plots were the same, and they persuaded me that I could become whatever I wanted to be. But come to think of it, they didn't enable me to become a good athlete! Somehow their message didn't register with my poorly coordinated body. I could have read Mr. Alger sixteen hours a day and it wouldn't have transformed me into a major league baseball player. I think of that when I read the story of this timid soul, and I feel sorry for him.

Even though I feel sorry for this one-talent man, he is the villain of the parable—not because he had only one talent, but because he wouldn't use what he had. Jesus is telling us that although life may be tough and may seem unfair, God is fair. We don't all have the same number or quality of talents, but we'll be judged only by what we do with what we have. God won't ask me why I didn't play centerfield as did Joe DiMaggio, but he will ask me if I became what Ellsworth Kalas was capable of becoming.

The timid soul doesn't look like a villain, because we have such stylistic ideas of what our villains should look like. Anyone who wastes life is a villain. Some waste it in obvious ways, like the prodigal in a far country. Most of us waste it in "socially acceptable" ways, which bring us no reproach.

Nothing is more valuable than life itself, and nothing is more tragic or more evil than to destroy life, whether in ourselves or in another. The thousand-dollar talent in the parable is nothing compared with the grand wealth of life God entrusts to each of us. To waste such a divine investment is serious business.

Contrary to our instinctive reaction—the employer was very generous. He trusted each of his workers with a substantial sum, asking only that they see what they could earn with it while he was gone. As far as we can see, he didn't tell them how to invest the money, and apparently he put no significant restrictions on them. They were left on their own, with marvelous freedom and a generous resource.

That's the way it is with all of us. Every human being begins with a gold coin, a life to be lived. The size of the coin varies according to the circumstances of life into which we are born, the abilities invested in us, and the setting in which we live out our lives. But we're all given a gold coin. We are given life itself, yet most of us never realize what a wonderful coin it is. Now and then we have a burst of insight, when we see how beautiful and special life is, but most of the time we toss about our gold coin in rather haphazard fashion, never calculating its worth.

The employer in Jesus' parable asked only one thing of his workers, that they earn something with the gold he had given them. The inference seems to be that the earning ought to be commensurate with the amount we've received. Thus the five-coin person brought back five more and was commended, as did the two-coin person. It seems clear that the one-coin man would have been praised with as much enthusiasm if only he had brought back a single coin.

Like the employer, God asks only one thing for giving us the gold of life: *Earn something with it.* Use what you have for a purpose.

The parable doesn't give an obvious spiritual directive. We're not told to pray, to be honest, to love God, or even to be kind to our neighbors. It seems simply to say, *Use, in the best way you can, what the King has entrusted to you.* You and I can go on to conclude that we'll never put our lives to the best use until we point them toward eternity and live with eternity in view, and we would be right. But the parable doesn't tell us that. It simply asks, "How are you going to use your gold coin?" And, "What do you owe the King who has entrusted you with such an inexpressibly valuable gift?"

At this point we begin to see why the timid soul is a villain. Or, in more theological terms, we begin to look more critically at our definition of sin. We're inclined to define sin in matters obviously of the flesh, or in the classic trinity of "thought, word, and deed." But perhaps the sin most to be feared, the one so easy to beset us, is our failure to trust God. The landowner believed in his servant enough to trust them with gold, but the timid soul didn't believe in himself that much, nor did he believe in the landowner's opinion of him.

J. B. Phillips, the Anglican rector who gave us such a special translation of the New Testament, disagreed sharply with this line from a familiar hymn: "O to be nothing, nothing . . ." Dr. Phillips said he searched the New Testament in vain to find an endorsement for that point of view. If ever a book taught people to be "something, something," he said, and to stand and do battle—"to be far more full of joy and daring and life than they ever were without God—that book is the New Testament!"[4]

How can we claim to believe in heaven if we have so little regard for the potential of life in the here and now? Perhaps there is no better way to prove that we cherish the prospect of eternity than to take hold of life on this earth with a passion and a gladness. Those who wrap their gold in a napkin and bury it, while they think of the world to come, show that they don't have much regard for eternity, because they have so little regard for time.

So the timid soul for whom I feel so sorry is, in truth, a villain. And the villain I see in him too often shows himself in me. On dark days of self-doubt (which are likely to be those days when I doubt the goodness of God), in times when weariness shuts out the sunlight of vigor and hope, or at times when I've simply lost heart, I bury the gold. Usually it's only for a brief period. But if life is such a precious thing, then why do I bury it for even a brief time? Sadly, some people bury the gold for all of their days—not because they're bad or because they hate God, but simply because they, like the timid soul in Jesus' story, are *afraid.*

I want to do something for that timid soul, partly because I have a picture in my memory of good but inadequate people who are somewhat beaten by life, who can't imagine themselves as winners. They've lost so often for so many years that they can't conceive of winning. I want to help those persons who are so timid about life and so doubtful of God and of themselves. I want to see them break free from their sense of worthlessness or helplessness, so they might fulfill the confidence shown in them by the One who entrusted them with their gold.

God's vision for us as workers ought to deliver every timid soul, for now and for eternity.

CHAPTER 4

The Seasons of the Soil

MATTHEW 13:1-9, 18-23: That same day Jesus went out of the house and sat beside the sea. Such great crowds gathered around him that he got into a boat and sat there, while the whole crowd stood on the beach. And he told them many things in parables, saying: "Listen! A sower went out to sow. And as he sowed, some seeds fell on the path, and the birds came and ate them up. Other seeds fell on rocky ground, where they did not have much soil, and they sprang up quickly, since they had no depth of soil. But when the sun rose, they were scorched; and since they had no root, they withered away. Other seeds fell among thorns, and the thorns grew up and choked them. Other seeds fell on good soil and brought forth grain, some a hundredfold, some sixty, some thirty. Let anyone with ears listen!". . .

"Hear then the parable of the sower. When anyone hears the word of the kingdom and does not understand it, the evil one comes and snatches away what is sown in the heart; this is what was sown on the path. As for what was sown on rocky ground, this is the one who hears the word and immediately receives it with joy; yet such a person has no root, but endures only for a while, and when trouble or persecution arises on account of the word, that person immediately falls away. As for what was sown among thorns, this is the one who hears the word, but the cares of the world and the lure of wealth choke the word, and it yields nothing. But as for what was sown on good soil, this is the one who hears the word and understands it, who indeed bears fruit and yields, in one case a hundredfold, in another sixty, and in another thirty."

I glanced through an old magazine of mine one day while riding a bus downtown. The first article intrigued me. I not only read it with interest, but I also began underlining passages at length.

Then, on page four, I came upon some underlined passages that I had marked several years before, when I had read the magazine for the first time.

Somehow, during my first reading, I hadn't found anything interesting enough in three pages to underline. In fact, my first impression was so slight that I didn't recognize that I had even seen the piece.

How is it that an article which once made no impression on me could later be so compelling? The answer is simple: I am several people—not in the sense that it would interest a psychiatrist, but in the sense that what leaves me cold today may set my soul aflame next week.

Usually when we read the parable of the sower, we think of the places on which the seed falls as descriptions of different types of persons. That's probably what Jesus had in mind when he told the story. But there's another side to the story. It describes, with unsettling accuracy, the several stages in the life of any person—you, me, Mother Teresa, or Adolf Hitler. The soil of which we human beings are made has seasons, and the seasons of our soil have everything to do with the way we handle the issues of life and eternity.

It's wonderfully appropriate that Jesus used the analogy of the sower, seed, and soil to portray the communication of the message of the Kingdom. One of the creation stories describes God making us from the dust of the earth and then breathing into us the breath of life. It's a marvelously graphic insight which points out that we human creatures are, indeed, dust, so that "to dust we shall return," and that this human soil is inhabited by the very breath of God.

So, yes—we are soil. From our very creation, such is our nature. But we are soil which is particularly hospitable to an eternal message, because the spirit of God is in us. Jesus' parable suggests that our soil has at least four different *seasons*.

In some cases, Jesus said, the seed of the kingdom falls "along the path," where "the birds come and eat it up." When the disciples asked Jesus to explain the meaning of his parable he said, "When anyone hears the word of the kingdom and does not understand it, the evil one comes and snatches away what is sown in the heart."

Sometimes I have been that kind of soil. It's difficult to recognize this kind of soil condition, because when our soil is like a beaten path, the seed survives so briefly that we may not even be conscious of its failing to germinate . . . at least, not until later.

I'm fascinated that when people come to know God well enough to be sensitive to their spiritual pilgrimage, they almost always begin to recall all sorts of encounters with God, which, at the time they happened, had not made any significant impression—or so it seemed. A middle-aged woman remembers that when she was just a small girl she had such a special moment at the time her grandmother died. "I don't know that I thought much of it at the time," she explains. "You know how children are. [One wants to interject, "Yes, and adults, too!"] In fact, I haven't thought of it in years. But now I can see that God was speaking to me even then." He was, indeed. Seed was falling on soil where the birds plucked it up before it could even find a place of lodging. No matter. A time comes when even the slightest, most fleeting impression is recalled.

Some writers say that the seed that falls "along the path" is that which is deflected from its purpose by the hardness of life. The figure of speech "along the path" suggests as much. When we think of a path on which so many have walked, we picture a person now world-weary. The author of Ecclesiastes, and all his spiritual descendants, comes to mind—those people who look at their books written, their romances experienced, their things accumulated and say bitterly, "Vanity, vanity, everything is vanity." I've heard some preachers (perhaps even myself) describe the hardness of this roadlike life: "Trodden upon by heartbreak, materialism, disappointment, and disillusionment, the soil is now so hard that even God's spirit cannot penetrate it."

Well, perhaps. But that isn't how Jesus described the people who are in this season. He characterized them for his disciples by saying that they are the kind of people who, upon hearing the message, do not understand it. And because there is no understanding, the seed never has opportunity to take lodging.

The season of not understanding can come at any point in life, for any number of reasons. It may, in particular, be part of the experience of childhood. But that's no reason to postpone sowing seed with children, saying impatiently, "Oh, she's too young to understand." In truth, most of us never know when someone is ready. This soil of ours is so complex and so unpredictable! Moreover, what we do not "understand" intellectually, we often store away in some corner of the psyche where it eventually finds its way into our conscious intellect. C. S. Lewis said that it was his imagination that was first converted, and that the other elements of his person followed.

Sometimes we choose not to understand. God forbid that I should be cynical or despairing after a lifetime of preaching, but I wonder if some of those people who, through the years, looked up at me with glazed eyes didn't long before make up their minds not to hear. Perhaps some of us preachers did it to them. They might have come to church wanting to hear, but after being disappointed too many Sundays, they simply decided it wasn't worth the effort. In time, bad preaching makes bad listeners, and goodness knows some people have heard a lot of bad preaching over the years! Others may have concluded that it is easier to lower their perception, because when they understand, their conscience tells them they ought to do something about themselves. It is better, therefore, not to understand!

This conclusion fits well with Jesus' explanation: "The evil one comes and snatches away what was sown in his heart." In other words, the evil one takes advantage of those circumstances which make it difficult for us to understand. When Mary Magdalene and the other women told the eleven what they had seen and experienced, the men "did not believe the women, because their words seemed to them like nonsense."[1] It's ironic, isn't it, that we can limit our understanding by the intellectual barriers we raise! Often, the mind has no greater enemy in the pursuit of knowledge than the mind itself, with its prejudices and prior certainties.

In any event, we have those seasons in life when our soil simply does not receive the seed. We do not understand, for one reason or another—perhaps because of the state of our lives at the time, or because of the way we've been conditioned, or because we haven't reached a point where we can hear as we should. So the enemy takes advantage of our season, snatching the seed away before any measurable impression is made. Nevertheless, we may at some later point in life discover that our psyches received at least some impression from the seed when it fell. Perhaps that's what the prophet had in mind when he promised that God's word will not return void, but that it will accomplish the purpose to which God has sent it.[2]

Other times, Jesus said, the seed of the Kingdom falls on rocky ground, where the soil is shallow. Sometimes our soil is shallow. It is not the kind of shallowness that makes us reject the message, but the kind that greets it with a short-lived enthusiasm.

Some people seem to be shallow all their lives. I know folks who constantly skip from one enthusiasm to another. In a sense, they're amusing. Whatever has captured their interest at the moment is always the best, the greatest, the "I've never seen anything like it before." Those who know such people know better than to take them too seriously. One wonders how they continue to be this way through the years.

But even the most conventional and stable persons have their periods of shallow enthusiasm. In every new-member class or any group of converts, there are some who will be gone within a few weeks, or at the most, months. The fact is, the soil is apt to be rather thin for most newcomers or new converts. And, sometimes, the greater the enthusiasm, the more shallow (or, perhaps, the more sensitive) the soil.

Some, however, will return later. Sometimes they make no reference to their brief stint. In other cases they may say, somewhat shamefacedly, "I guess I just wasn't ready at the time." It may be just that simple: a matter of timing, of the seasons of the soil.

Jesus explained this shallowness as a failing that happens "when trouble or persecution comes." In our culture, religious persecution isn't likely to be very intense, but it's enough to discourage some. In some cases, there's a kind of persecution in reverse. People enter the fellowship of the church with high expectations—as they ought—and find that, after a short period of warm welcome, they're left much to themselves or are even made to feel that it will be a while before they'll belong to the inner circle of the congregation.

Is there an age when the soil of the soul is more inclined to be shallow? Probably. Certainly teens are susceptible to quick and easy enthusiasms; they always have been. Puberty inclines us that way. When a person's body is going through all sorts of strange and inexplicable changes, one should be forgiven for becoming easy prey to new possibilities and for not holding to them for long.

This problem is, no doubt, intensified today. Teenagers, more than most of us, are influenced by their peers. Youth culture raises up new heroes and fads almost as quickly as public relations offices can pump out new promotional materials. Some of them hardly seem to get Andy Warhol's designated fifteen minutes of fame, but their popularity usually lasts long enough to sell fifty thousand T-shirts.

And so it is that young people make commitments at youth camp or at a Christian musical extravaganza, only to be preoccupied with other interests before the month is out. We are like that in our adolescent years. Interests come and go with astonishing rapidity. Our enthusiasms awaken easily and die just as quickly. Our soil is shallow. In a sense, this is part of the charm of the young. It is also, at times, a cause for despair.

But this, too, is a generalization, and it should not make for prejudicial judgments. Many young people are as consistent as aged saints. I've known some with more maturity than the Administrative Board that gravely wonders what is happening to the young people. Nevertheless, if there is any age in life when we are susceptible to shallowness or to passing enthusiasms it is when we are in our teens.

Another time when the soil of the soul is inclined to be shallow is in periods of personal loneliness. When people are lonely, they are more apt to grasp at emotional straws. That's why the widow is easy prey for the confidence game or the religious charlatan. The soil is quick to entertain some new seed, since the soil has been disrupted by loss. At such times a person is also very open to religious experience. But the soil may well be lacking in depth, and the plant which springs up so quickly may just as quickly wither away.

Jesus also said that, sometimes, the seed of the Kingdom falls among thorns. If there is a season of soil of which we should be most aware, it is the season when the seed is sown among thorns. This is the person who hears the word, but who lets "the worries of this life and the deceitfulness of wealth choke it." There is no age at which we are immune to this peril—every age has its distracting toys—but we are probably most susceptible between the ages of twenty and forty-five. These are the years when life is full of excitements: career, courtship, and for some, marriage and the starting of family, as well as the challenge of establishing a sound financial base for eventual retirement. If these "weeds" don't choke out the best of God's seed, nothing will.

This is a harsh word. I have classified many good things (indeed, my whole list is made up of good things!) as weeds. But in doing so, I've been true to the gospel. That which distracts us from the best becomes, by that very fact, a weed. I am not doing violence to the parable when I find significant that it provides only two categories, the kingdom of seed and weed. There is no provision for "other nice plants." This is what Jesus was saying when he warned us that we must be ready to hate father and mother, wife and children, brothers and sisters, and our own life in order to be a true disciple.[3] Tear up all these "good things," the Master seems to be saying, because if you don't, they will choke out the seed of the Kingdom.

On the surface, that seems a brutal judgment. But it is so only in the manner of the surgeon who inflicts a pain so that he or she can save a life. If we wish to keep—*truly* keep—father and mother, spouse and children, brothers and sisters, and our own lives, we need to get our priorities in order so that life can be saved.

There's an exceeding irony in this portion of Jesus' story. If there is any soil that holds great promise, other than the soil in the latter part of the story, which brings forth life so abundantly, it is this soil wherein the weeds and thorns take over. That's why the thorns find it so hospitable. The qualities that make it attractive to life's choking elements are the very qualities that would, under better circumstances, make it magnificently productive.

So it is with all our lives. When the soil of our souls is at its best potential, we are so often preoccupied with other things. In the years when we are capable of our greatest productivity, we are most easily taken over by weeds.

Finally, there are the seasons of good soil. Some people never seem, on the surface, to have such times. All of us feel, on our worst days, that we aren't capable of having such times. Nineteenth-century poet and novelist George Macdonald, whose writings first turned C. S. Lewis toward God and of whom Lewis said, "I know hardly any other writer who seems closer, or more continually close, to the Spirit of Christ himself," sometimes thought the soil of his own soul was hopeless.

> My soul is a poor land, plenteous in dearth—
> Here blades of grass, there a small herb for food—
> A nothing that would be something if it could.[4]

I understand such a mood, and perhaps you can, too. My soil is often, it seems, "a nothing that would be something if it could." But the Master held out hope for your soil and mine. We are capable, he said, of bringing forth thirty, sixty, and a hundredfold.

The soil that is so resistant that birds carry away the seed before it takes root, or so shallow that a sprout springs up and dies within a day, or so encumbered with itself that its weeds choke out the seed of the Kingdom, is also the soil that can bring forth abundantly. I believe there are seasons in the soil of the soul. Yours and mine. I dare not, therefore, give up hope for any soil. Especially for my own. If I give up hope for your soil, I will hurt you, no doubt about it, but I can't finally destroy you. I am capable, however, of destroying myself. We are our own worst enemies. That's why it is so important for us to know the potential of the soil of our souls, and to know that we are fully able to bring forth abundantly for the Eternal Farmer.

Are there times when we are more likely to be instruments of goodness, just as there seem to be times when we are more likely to be unproductive? Most students of human psychology would say yes. We're often told, for instance, that a large percentage of people decide to follow Christ when they are eleven, twelve, and thirteen years old. If during those years we are especially inclined to quick enthusiasms, then we are also inclined to grand decisions, as many of us will testify. The decisions may be immature, shallow, and naive, but often the best choices of our lives come at just such times. The kingdom of heaven is made of such stuff.

There are other seasons when the soil of the soul may be particularly open to productivity. In the days when Fulton Sheen was one of the most popular figures on television and was converting many to Christianity, he was asked in an interview to explain the secret of his conversions. He answered, with great insight, that his converts came to their decision in times of personal crisis. Bereavement, severe illness, the loss of a friendship, or the breaking up of a marriage, a time of personal defeat—all of these may provide soil in which the soul becomes richly sensitive.

For some, life's later years produce good soul soil. In most cases, however, this is more likely if the person has had times of real openness to God in earlier years. Not many people become profoundly spiritual in old age if they have been crudely materialistic throughout their earlier years. The child and the young adult almost always are the parent of the elder soul.

No rule holds for everybody, however. We are as different in our spiritual responses as in our fingerprints. The seasons of a person's soil are not amenable to rigid structures. They happen as life happens. Devise a neat theory for the soil of the soul and tomorrow someone will disprove it with his or her experience. There are moments in life, thanks be to God, when we are startlingly sensitive. Sometimes the moments are explicable; sometimes not.

Leslie Weatherhead, one of the most popular preachers in twentieth-century England, told of a time during the First World War when he was riding horseback in the deserts of Mesopotamia on a government errand. He was so preoccupied that he hardly knew which day of the week it was. He rode into a camp where a service was being held in a YMCA tent. He recalled, "I was tired and hot and dusty but, though I can't remember even the name of the preacher, I *knew* that Christ had forgiven my sins, that he was there and that he loved me."[5] It was not, by usual judgments, a spiritually propitious moment, yet it was for him a moment when the soil of the soul was uniquely fertile.

Those who love the souls of men and women do well to remember this. Whenever we serve as witnesses to the faith, we must do so with all earnestness, because one doesn't know the season in which some soul currently abides. That uninterested, distracted, or unresponsive person may be nearer the Kingdom than we—or they—realize.

The truth of it is, we dare not give up on anyone, at any time—including ourselves. The ancient wisdom writer said there were three things too amazing for him and four things that he could not understand. I would add a fifth, the most wondrous of all: the seasons of the soil of the human soul.

CHAPTER 5

The Sad Story of the Embarrassed Farmers

MATTHEW 13:24-30, 36-43: He put before them another parable: "The kingdom of heaven may be compared to someone who sowed good seed in his field; but while everybody was asleep, an enemy came and sowed weeds among the wheat, and then went away. So when the plants came up and bore grain, then the weeds appeared as well. And the slaves of the householder came and said to him, 'Master, did you not sow good seed in your field? Where, then, did these weeds come from?' He answered, 'An enemy has done this.' The slaves said to him, 'Then do you want us to go and gather them?' But he replied, 'No; for in gathering the weeds you would uproot the wheat along with them. Let both of them grow together until the harvest; and at harvest time I will tell the reapers, Collect the weeds first and bind them in bundles to be burned, but gather the wheat into my barn.'"

. . . Then he left the crowds and went into the house. And his disciples approached him, saying, "Explain to us the parable of the weeds of the field." He answered, "The one who sows the good seed is the Son of Man; the field is the world, and the good seed are the children of the kingdom; the weeds are the children of the evil one, and the enemy who sowed them is the devil; the harvest is the end of the age, and the reapers are angels. Just as the weeds are collected and burned up with fire, so will it be at the end of the age. The Son of Man will send his angels, and they will collect out of his kingdom all causes of sin and all evildoers, and they will throw them into the furnace of fire, where there will be weeping and gnashing of teeth. Then the righteous will shine like the sun in the kingdom of their Father. Let anyone with ears listen!"

Nothing is as embarrassing to the Christian church as its hypocrites. When our critics attack us at this point, we can explain, but we cannot deny. I remember from my boyhood the evangelist who said, "Sin! You can hear the hiss of the serpent in the very word." One can say "Hypocrisy" with the same emphasis and conclusion.

No wonder, then, that Jesus told a story dealing with the issue of hypocrisy. He didn't identify it as a parable about hypocrites, but, for that matter, Jesus rarely identified the theme of a story. Master teacher and storyteller that he was, he left that to us.

There was a great landowner, Jesus said, who wanted to make the most of his holdings. He purchased the best possible seed to guarantee a good return from his land. But he had an enemy. One night while his workers were sleeping, the enemy slipped into the field and sowed noxious weeds everywhere, right in the midst of the grain.

In time, of course, the crime became evident, as weeds appeared in the field. In their weed-like way, they began taking over the field. The workers sought advice from their employer: Shall we uproot the weeds, they asked, and cast them out? No, the landowner cautioned; if you do, you may tear up some of the grain with the weeds. Wait till the harvest time. When everything is full-grown, we will gather up the weeds and burn them; then we'll harvest the grain.

The basic meaning of the parable seems clear enough, but the apostles asked for an explanation. They asked for an explanation as we would ask someone for clarification because we can hardly believe our ears, even though it's pretty obvious what the other party has in mind. So Jesus explained that the field is the world and the landowner is Jesus, who has sown the good seed, the children of the Kingdom. The weeds are the "children of the evil one," and the enemy who sows them is the devil. This is the state of our world: It is a place where good grain and weeds grow together—where, in fact, they are often so intermixed and perhaps even so indistinguishable that judgment cannot be made until the day of final reckoning.

I identify with that anonymous group in the story described as slaves or servants. Although the householder—the Son of Man—is said to have sown the good seed, he, in truth, has only directed the project. The servants are the actual functionaries. I sense their apprehension as they report the problem to their master. They fear either that they have done something wrong or that the householder will judge them responsible for the sorry state of the field. "How could this happen?" they ask, all the while fearing it is their fault.

During my years as a pastor, I have sometimes approached the Great Householder with just such apprehension. I've sown good seed, or so it seems to me, but now look at the results! How can these things be? How is it that my earnest efforts have produced these half-hearted followers? The program chair in the women's organization has the same problem. She has planned a program that will stir spiritual renewal in her group, she's sure. But several members can hardly wait for the program to end so that they can pick up their complaint that "we have to find some way to keep other people from using the church kitchen." So it is with the youth counselors who plan an overnight retreat which they think will transform their group, only to discover they spend most of the night contending with teenage boys who are trying to sneak out of their quarters and teenage girls who hope the boys succeed. How could our good sowing, our careful planning, our earnest praying, go astray? Is it our fault, Master?

Well, probably, at times. But, on the whole, Jesus has a very pragmatic view. "An enemy has done this," he says. That is, this is the way things are. This is the kind of world we're in and the kind of battle in which we're engaged. There's an enemy, and you might as well be reconciled to that fact and work accordingly.

Don't break your heart over the weeds, farmer! Weeds are a post-Eden fact of life.

But we farmers see it differently. We'll get rid of those blasted weeds. Sometimes we seek to do so by the rules we set up. Some Protestant denominations have insisted that no one can become part of their fellowship who uses tobacco or alcohol or who participates in "worldly amusements," such as dancing or attending movies. These are easily measurable ways of keeping the seed and the consequent harvest pure, at least by our judgment.

Others have sought to keep the seed and harvest pure by enforcing doctrinal purity. Only those who subscribe to rigidly defined statements of belief are allowed to join the church. That, too, is calculated to keep the weeds out.

Still others seek a perfect field by keeping their farm small. They choose to have a tightly knit congregation where there can be careful supervision not only by the pastor but also by one another. But these groups have long since proved to have their own built-in problems.

Their smallness easily makes them inbred and exclusive, with a sense of superiority to the "others" outside.

In the classic language of the comic strip character Pogo, "We have met the enemy, and he is us." Who am I to throw out my sister or brother? My very discernment in making such a decision is colored by *my* sinfulness. I have no business tearing up another plant, for my judgment is faulted in so many ways. This rooting up and sorting out is a work for angels.

That's the answer I give when people come to me with this question that seems to enchant many: "Do you think a person can go to heaven if . . . thus and so?" I rejoice that I am not in the position to make such judgments. In many instances I know what the scriptures say, but I must confess that my interpretation of those scriptures may be highly fallible. The truth is, I myself am a bit of a weed. How can I judge the quality of others?

Jesus warned that in gathering the weeds we would "uproot the wheat along with them." I've seen that happen in the simplest ways, such as when a pastor who is anxious to clean up the church rolls removes the names of persons long inactive and, by his or her logic, justifiably removed. But it is not justified in the eyes of a loving parent or sibling! I've come upon a number of persons over the years who have allowed themselves to be alienated from a particular congregation or pastor—and sometimes from the community of faith as a whole—because someone they love was removed from the church rolls by a zealous roll keeper.

But there's a still more significant factor. Every analogy has its limitations, and the limitation here is that people are not plants. Wheat is always wheat and a weed is always a weed, but not so with people. The person I think a weed today may prove, somewhere down the road, to be a better plant than I am. In my zeal to clean up the field I may be highly premature in my judgment. What looks today like a weed may in truth be nothing other than an immature blade of wheat. Give it time, farmer! More important, don't let your pride in the quality of your farming destroy your understanding of the Great Householder's grace.

I wish the matter of hypocrisy were as simple as the critics seem to think. Almost anyone can recognize the man who makes pious protestations on Sunday but with whom one would be afraid to enter a business deal on weekdays, and the woman who smiles sweetly to outsiders but is a terror of unpleasantness in her own home. Such weeds are easy to identify.

Even in such instances the attending farmer must be cautious in his or her judgment. Only God knows the base of character and personality from which we work. When I'm ready to pass judgment on another's shortcomings, I try to remind myself of the story of two Civil War generals in the heat of battle. One, noticing the perspiration of fear on the brow of his comrade, said, "Sir, if I were as frightened as you, I'd be ashamed to wear our uniform." And the other replied, "Sir, if you were as frightened as I am, you would have fled the field of battle by now." We never know the personal equipment with which other people labor, nor the struggles they experience while simply staying alive. Even the most obvious weeds deserve compassion or renewed understanding.

The more serious problem for those who think they can be rid of the weeds is in our very fallible human judgment. In the Middle East there is a kind of weed that, especially in its early stages, looks so much like wheat that not even a master farmer can distinguish one from the other. No doubt this was the plant Jesus had in mind in his parable, and it surely applies to our situation in our typical middle-class churches.

So many of the characteristics of Christianity are found in conventional middle-class life. It's probably an unspoken tribute to Christianity that secular society in the Western world has taken on many of the dimensions of the Christian life-style without really intending to be Christian. So it is that the average "nice" person wants to be a good neighbor who maintains a pleasant relationship with everyone (or nearly everyone), while being involved in good causes. Some people will confess, pragmatically, that they've learned that this kind of life-style pays, because it makes one successful, helps in seeking public office or the presidency of a service club. No wonder some of the ethical teachings of the Christian faith have become almost synonymous with Western culture. If the cross is left out of the story, both as a means of redemption and as a way of life, then suburban gentility is almost indistinguishable from our traditional image of the Christian life.

This is an especially difficult problem when, unconsciously, we associate Christianity with particular culture patterns. We smile at those nineteenth-century missionaries who insisted on introducing

Western dress and mores to natives as part of their conversion, but we are their kin more often than we want to recognize. A great many church people find their sense of community with others not on the basis of Christian commitment or the fruit of the Spirit, but according to their taste in music, literature, drama, art, and fashion. There are quite sincere suburbanites who (though they would find it hard to confess even to themselves) can't imagine a Christian who would wear white socks with a suit.

It works the other way, too. Some people at another point of the economic and social scale quite easily write off the Christianity of people who dress well and have "uppity ways." They remind one and all that Jesus was a carpenter, not an executive, and that a rich person will find it very hard to enter the Kingdom—not realizing that their judgment, too, is colored by their social outlook.

I'm glad it's not my business to clear the rolls of the kingdom of God. The great preacher Clovis Chappell loved to say that everyone has a right to enter the kingdom of heaven, but no one has a right to shut anyone else out. We need to remember that our judgment in these matters is made fallible by our own social, intellectual, and personal preconceptions, and we can't hope to eliminate all those prejudices in our judging of others. We do well, therefore, to stay out of the judging business, just as Jesus recommended.

This parable can also be applied, in a measure, to our individual souls. The field is my soul. A great deal of seed is sown there, some of it by my choosing and some when I'm "asleep"—that is, distracted enough that I'm not really conscious of what's happening. We take a fair bit of bad seed into our persons with our eyes wide open, but some of it is sown when our defenses are down. I think of an earnest Christian Scientist who told me he wouldn't listen to those television commercials that pushed patent medicines, because they were often so graphic, depicting headaches and stomach upsets, that they tilted one toward illness. His point is well taken, and so it is with a large amount of the material that enters our "field" every day, by way of radio, television, and casual conversation. Bad seed is sown and we often welcome it unwittingly.

No wonder, then, that "when I would do good, evil is present with me."[1] This field of mine is so susceptible to all kinds of planting. And no wonder that when I look for the fruit of the Spirit in my life, I often find a good bit of stuff of which I'm ashamed. Sometimes I know how it got there; I planted it myself, careless farmer that I am! But sometimes it was sown during the night, and I'm bitterly disturbed that it has become part of the crop of my person.

The phrase from daily speech, "work like the devil," has some basis, it seems. Evil works nights. But evil also works days. If only the devil would show himself with tail and pitchfork, as in a book I remember from my childhood, I'd do a better job of resisting. But the Bible reminds us that he sometimes "disguises himself as an angel of light."[2] He appears in some of the best places, and at some of the most unlikely times. And he seems never to sleep.

As a Christian, I'm troubled by the way weeds are sown in my life, and as a professional church worker, I'm troubled by the prominence of weeds in the church and the embarrassment they cause us through those who accuse us of hypocrisy. Is there anything we can do to improve this situation?

For one thing, I need to remind myself that I may often, perhaps without realizing it, be sowing mixed seed. Those of us who try to serve Christ, both clergy and laity, are imperfect souls with mixed motives. As a matter of fact, if God used us only when our motives were pure, heaven's work would never begin.

I'm often appalled by the self-seeking and personal ambition of the clergy. I'm troubled that in so many instances they act as if churches exist to provide them with careers rather than as if they are called to serve the church and the people. The striving for recognition and for personal advancement are as strong in the church, it seems, as in any secular vocation. I'm also troubled to find that, with all my sensitivity to these evils in others, they still find lodging at times in my own soul.

It's quite possible that we clergy sow mixed seed because we ourselves are mixed. So it is with lay involvement in the church. Sometimes we even cater to misplaced ambition by extending special recognition to the "top givers" in the church. Without a doubt, many people accept church offices because of the prestige they find in being a trustee or the power that accrues in being part of the committee that chooses or dismisses church staff.

When our motives are mixed, we can hardly expect to sow only good seed. When Jesus identified the enemy as the devil, he didn't say how the devil would go about this work of infiltration; but it seems that just as the good done in our world is usually done through human instruments, so too the evil will come through us as human beings. There's no reason to doubt that some of the evil seed sown in God's field is laid there by those of us who claim to be God's workers. No wonder the farmer is embarrassed. He has reason to be.

To be effective, the farmer needs also to remember a very encouraging fact about the project in which we are engaged: The enemy is an intruder. This field belongs to God. Whether the field is the church, the whole world, or the individual human soul, it is God's field, not the devil's. The enemy is an intruder, an interloper, a latecomer. He may make a strong claim to this world and its inhabitants, but he has no primary rights.

This world belongs to God. His is the field, the seed, the workers. We need to remember this when the power of evil is so insistent that we think we are helpless before its assault. Mark Twain once said that the devil must be a pretty admirable fellow to have got so large a percentage of the human race to respond to him. Well, he was not here first, and he will not be here last. The ultimate power is God's, for this is his planet. We sometimes-beleaguered farmers of faith need to remember this, lest we lose the harvest by default.

In that same vein, we need to remember that the whole world is not "going to the devil" just because there are weeds in the field. The workers in Jesus' parable seemed to feel all was lost, or at least in great peril, because they found darnel weeds in their fields. You and I often respond the same way. We read of corruption in politics and quickly decide there's not an honest person left in the world of politics. Or we hear of a religious leader who has exploited the people in order to live in scandalous luxury, and we forget about the hundreds of thousands of religious workers who live modestly or in sacrificial poverty.

There are, indeed, weeds in the field of this world, of the church, and of our own lives. But that doesn't mean the cause of goodness is lost. Maltbie Babcock was right in reminding us

> that though the wrong seems oft so strong,
> God is the ruler yet.[3]

Give time, the Great Landowner said, because in time there will be a reckoning, and we'll be able to separate the weeds from the grain.

Meanwhile, you and I need to work at the task of goodness as earnestly and as untiringly as the enemy works at the business of evil.

And we need to be knowledgeable about his evil ways, lest we be party to his purposes.

Through it all, we dare not lose heart. For though the enemy is clever and fearsomely industrious, he cannot finally win. This is our Father's world, and if we work with him, we are on the winning side. The harvest will come, and it will be right.

CHAPTER 6

Love Always Wins . . . Sometimes

LUKE 15:11-32: Then Jesus said, "There was a man who had two sons. The younger of them said to his father, 'Father, give me the share of the property that will belong to me.' So he divided his property between them. A few days later the younger son gathered all he had and traveled to a distant country, and there he squandered his property in dissolute living. When he had spent everything, a severe famine took place throughout that country, and he began to be in need. So he went and hired himself out to one of the citizens of that country, who sent him to his fields to feed the pigs. He would gladly have filled himself with the pods that the pigs were eating; and no one gave him anything. But when he came to himself he said, 'How many of my father's hired hands have bread enough and to spare, but here I am dying of hunger! I will get up and go to my father, and I will say to him, "Father, I have sinned against heaven and before you; I am no longer worthy to be called your son;

treat me like one of your hired hands."' So he set off and went to his father. But while he was still far off, his father saw him and was filled with compassion; he ran and put his arms around him and kissed him. Then the son said to him, 'Father, I have sinned against heaven and before you; I am no longer worthy to be called your son.' But the father said to his slaves, 'Quickly, bring out a robe—the best one—and put it on him; put a ring on his finger and sandals on his feet. And get the fatted calf and kill it, and let us eat and celebrate; for this son of mine was dead and is alive again; he was lost and is found!' And they began to celebrate.

"Now his elder son was in the field; and when he came and approached the house, he heard music and dancing. He called one of the slaves and asked what was going on. He replied, 'Your brother has come, and your father has killed the fatted calf, because he has got him back safe and sound.' Then he became angry and refused to go in. His father came out and began to plead with him. But he answered his father, 'Listen! For all these years I have been working like a slave for you, and I have never disobeyed your command; yet you have never given me even a young goat so that I might celebrate with my friends. But when this son of yours came back, who has devoured your property with prostitutes, you killed the fatted calf for him!' Then the father said to him, 'Son, you are always with me, and all that is mine is yours. But we had to celebrate and rejoice, because this brother of yours was dead and has come to life; he was lost and has been found.'"

*I*t sometimes seems that we spend the first ten or twelve years of our lives learning great rules, then spend the remainder of our years discovering exceptions to those rules. There's a story about this in the Bible. It's such a beloved story (perhaps my personal favorite in all of the Bible) that I hate to disturb its place in our hearts; but, if I am to be honest, I have no choice.

Everybody knows that love always wins. That's one of life's ultimate truisms. We impress it upon our children, and when we come upon some misanthrope who suggests otherwise, we're sure his or her supply of the milk of human kindness has gone badly sour.

Yet, like it or not, most of us—as time goes by—witness instances when love *doesn't* win. Or if love wins, the victory comes so late that it hardly matters. That's hard to accept. Having been nurtured in the faith that love always comes out on top, we try to ignore those times when it seems to work otherwise. But when we insist that love invariably wins, experience answers, "Only sometimes."

One day Jesus overheard some religious leaders criticizing him for associating with the "questionables" of society. He answered by telling them three stories. The last of the three is often said to be the most beautiful short story ever written.

A certain man, Jesus said, had two sons. On the surface, they were very different. The older son worked hard on the family farm. The younger son was restless. The family life-style often bored him, while the glamor of the distant city fascinated and enticed him.

One day the younger son asked his father if he could make an early claim on his inheritance. Let me have my share now, he said, so that I can test my wings and do my thing. The father, a generous man—perhaps unduly generous—agreed, and before long the boy headed off to the big city that he had dreamed of for so long.

Soon he was living in the fast lane. With his rather substantial inheritance, he found friends quickly, and they helped him find ways to spend his money. Before he knew it (almost overnight, it seemed) his money was gone. And not surprisingly, his new friends were gone, too. Now he was forced to scrape and struggle for a living. He was driven at last to feed pigs, the ugliest of jobs for a first-century Jew. As he fed the pigs, he envied them, for their diet was better than his. Then he came to his senses: "I'm going home" he said. "My father's servants live better than I do."

So home he went—weary, threadbare, sick of body, sick of himself, sick of life. "But when he was yet a great way off," his father saw him. That phrase, all by itself, lets us know how loving a man his father was. We can only conclude that the father had been waiting for his boy almost from the day he had left. So it was that he saw him while he was still "a great way off." And, believe me, that distant look is a measure of love.

Struggling and stumbling, the boy came. He had probably been gone no more than a year, but it was as if he were twenty years older. "Father," he wept, "I have sinned against heaven and before you; I am no longer worthy to be called your son." The father interrupted the confession with his own song of love and joy. "Get the best robe for this boy," he said to a servant. "Get a ring for his finger and shoes for his feet. Kill our best calf and set up a party. The boy I lost has returned! We're going to celebrate!"

It's a marvelous scene, the celebration of the victory of love. But it isn't the end of the story. I wish it were. As the party gained momentum, the older son came in from the fields. When he heard what was happening, he was bitterly angry. "You never had a party for me," he said to his father. "I've worked hard all these years, and you never did anything nice like this for me."

Again, the father responded with love. He tried to explain to his older son not only why he felt such joy in the younger son's return, but also of his depth of love for him, the older son.

But we never know whether the older son responded to his father's love. The story ends here, leaving the outcome uncertain. We don't know if love won. We hope so. Our sentimental longing for happy endings causes us to assume that surely love must have won. But neither Jesus nor the gospel writer ever tells us.

When we read this story or preach or teach it, we usually

concentrate on the boy who left home. That's natural, because his story is by far the most exciting. It's the sort of story that quickly gains our interest. Occasionally someone pays attention to the story of the older brother, as I shall do later. But there's another way to approach this story from the back side: from the point of view of the father.

We don't know his name, of course. Jesus almost never gave names to the characters in his parables, perhaps because names would have distracted his listeners from applying the parables to themselves. But for purposes of ease in storytelling, I will call the father Zachariah.

He was a loving father, even to the point of indulgence—the kind of father of whom neighbors might say, "He gives those kids too much for their own good." In this, he was—of course—like God, who has been so inexpressibly generous in his endowments to our human race. So it was with this man. Thus when his younger boy asked for an early inheritance, he indulged him. It probably wasn't the wise thing to do. The boy must have been terribly spoiled even to suggest such a thing, and the father only encouraged the boy's self-centeredness by giving him his way. I have a feeling this father often erred on the side of kindness.

Someone might say, "If you're going to err, isn't that the way to go? After all, you can't love too much, can you?" That's probably what the father said, too, provided he considered the matter philosophically. It's quite possible he didn't even think about it, that he was just doing what came naturally to him, without benefit of intensive self-examination.

I can imagine the conversations that took place in the nearby town, where the family was well known, when word got out that the father had given the younger son his inheritance. One townsman stopped another. "Did you hear what old Zach just did? He's giving his younger boy his share of the family estate. The kid doesn't know his head from a bunch of grapes, and now he's got all that money. Mark you, it will do him no good!"

A week or two went by, and some of the townspeople were talking again. "Hear the latest about Zachariah and his boys? The younger boy just left home."

"I'm not surprised," the neighbor answered. "Not surprised at all. I knew he'd do something like that the moment I heard about the fool thing Zach did with the inheritance. No sir, it doesn't surprise me at all. In fact, I think I told you that would happen, didn't I? Do you remember me telling you that?"

A month went by. "I was in the city last week," a man reported. "You can't guess what I saw. Old Zach's boy. I want to tell you, he was living it up. He had a blonde on one arm and a brunette on the other. Both good-lookers, too. He was about three sheets in the wind. I don't know much about clothes, but I can tell you he didn't buy his outfit in a discount store."

"You know what they say," his neighbor answered. "A fool and his money are soon parted. Zach should have known better than to give that boy his money. Zach is a good fellow, just as nice a fellow as you'll ever hope to find, but he's just too kind. Especially where his boys are concerned."

Six months went by. "Do you suppose Zach knows what's happened to his boy?" a man asked.

"What do you mean?"

"I mean the trouble he's gotten into. The fool kid's apparently spent all his money, every thin mite of it. And to make it worse, the bottom's fallen out of business in the city. Real estate's at a standstill and there's hardly a job to be found. A lot of businesses have closed down."

"Sure, sure. But what's happened to Zach's boy?"

"Well, a fellow saw him the other day. Samuel, I think it was. Said he looked like Skid Row revisited. Hardly enough rags to cover his hind quarters."

"What was he doing? Panhandling?"

"Worse. He was feeding pigs. Honest! And to tell you the truth, Sam said the boy looked like he envied the pigs their food."

The second man shook his head for a moment, then shifted his ever-present straw. "You know, it's hard to understand. Old Zach loved that boy so much—well, both of them, for that matter—and Zach's such a good man. But that fool kid of his has just gone to the devil. And as far as I can see, Zach's done nothing but right by him. It just makes you wonder what good it does to love somebody. It sure does make you wonder."

Then one morning there was a different kind of conversation. "Hear the good news about Zach and his younger boy?"

"Man, everybody's heard! Why, you could hear the orchestra playing halfway to town last night. I've never known the kind of celebration old Zach threw for his boy's homecoming."

"I'm sure glad for Zachariah. The boy is thin as a skeleton, but he looked happy. Glad to be home, I guess."

"It wasn't all good, though," the second man said. "Just as the party was going strong last night, the older boy came in from the fields. Always been hard feelings between the two boys, you know. They're so different, at least in some ways. Well, the older boy just wouldn't have anything to do with the party. I understand that old Zach stood outside and begged him to come in. They say he had tears in his eyes."

"Did the older boy ever go in?"

"I don't rightly know. My friend—the one who told me this part—felt embarrassed to listen any longer. He said Zachariah was just begging his boy, pleadin' with him to join the celebration."

"You know, the older one never has been much like his father. You wonder how he could grow up with an old man like his and still be as mean-spirited as he is. Mind you, he's honest and hard-working, but nothing like Zach. You just can't help wondering why Zach's boys haven't turned out better than they have. It sure isn't because they lacked love, I'll tell you that."

That's the question I leave with you on the father's behalf: Why doesn't love always win? A proverb often seen on Sunday school walls says that children become like what they live with: Let them live with anger and they grow up to be angry people, but let them live with love and they will grow up to be loving people. The odds are definitely with that philosophy. If you're a betting person, you can lay your bet on love producing love and hate producing hate.

Judging from what we know and see, however, love isn't a sure thing. Some people who grow up with love simply become spoiled. And some children whose parents are patient seem to grow up insistent and demanding, as if the patience of their parents had taught them that they can always get their own way if they only hold out long enough.

So it is in some friendships and marriages. Rather than learning unselfishness from the other, a partner seems to learn how to exploit the other person's good nature. People learn, as the saying goes, what buttons to push to get their own way. A philosophy of human relationships devised in recent years suggests that where there is an alcoholic, there likely is a family member or friend who helps that person to be or to continue to be an alcoholic; and where there's an abusive personality, there's someone who abets the abusiveness by unwitting compliance, to the point of cooperation.

Nevertheless, we wonder how the father in Jesus' parable, the man I've called Zachariah, could have two sons of the sort we've found in this story. The younger son was so selfish in his youthful days—until life painfully awakened him—that he sought his inheritance early, being indifferent to his father's feelings; and he was so foolish that he wasted it in drunken, lecherous living. Surely he didn't learn that kind of conduct from his father. And the older brother was so self-centered that he couldn't rejoice in his father's happiness. All he could think about was that he'd never had a party to compare with this one. His attitude and personality were so unlike his father's. Where did the father fail? How is it that his love, which is so apparent and so admirable, didn't win?

Well, love is risky. The outcome depends on the response of the other party. Worse yet, love has to work with that most unpredictable of creatures, the human being. If ever there were unprogrammed creatures, they are we! There may be buttons that we can push to get certain results from fellow human beings, but those buttons don't always work. We respond as we want to, buttons notwithstanding.

No wonder, then, that some parents operate by threat and by force. If you don't do what I say, they announce, you'll pay for it. That's a more effective control than love, but only in the short run; and, of course, it violates the very nature of a reasoned relationship.

With love, you have to depend on the response of the other person, and that's a gamble. Yet that's the way God has chosen to relate to this world of ours. God is the Father in the parable. How, then, does God feel when he looks out on all his sons and daughters? Does God sometimes say, Why haven't they responded properly to my love?

Apparently so. At least, that's the way the prophet Jeremiah saw it so many centuries ago. Speaking for God, Jeremiah said,

> What wrong did your fathers find in me
>   that they went far from me,
> and went after worthlessness, and became worthless?[1]

That is, why didn't they follow my example? How is it that they could observe my love and grace, then choose a shoddy, self-destructive way?

The prophet Hosea described the divine anguish in even more painful language. Like Jeremiah, speaking directly in God's stead, Hosea said:

> I took them [Israel] up in my arms;
> but they did not know that I healed them.
> I led them with cords of compassion,
> with the bands of love.[2]

But in their dullness of spirit, they didn't recognize who it was that had healed them, or who was caring for them, or that they were the beneficiaries of love.

Likewise, Jesus made the case with tears. Weeping over Jerusalem in the last days of his earthly life he said, "I would have gathered you the way a chicken gathers her little ones under her wings, and you would not."[3] Still, we do not see, and those of us who at least see enough that we identify ourselves with Christ's name are still so slow of understanding that we live much of the time as if we understood not.

Several years ago the writer Philip Yancey spent two winter weeks in a mountain cabin in Colorado, reading through his Bible. He began at Genesis and read straight through, trying to isolate himself to the Book for an intensive immersion in its fullness. As he concluded his reading, he was struck by the fact that the Bible is not a collection of decrees or a description of the divine attributes but is more a story of God, the Jilted Lover. As he felt the pain of the grand biblical story, Yancey asked himself, "Why would the God who created all that exists subject himself to such humiliation from his creation?"[4]

One would think God would have grown tired of loving our world, or that he would have given up on us. Instead, however, he keeps on believing in love and in us and in our potential to respond to love.

Love is a risky business, no doubt about it. In a sense, it's surprising that love ever succeeds, because love depends on such gentle, uncontrolling methods. Yet love's success record, though imperfect, is remarkably high. And the biggest recommendation for love is this: Love is the method God has chosen to use. If God believes in love so much, it's obviously worth trying.

So I suggest some guidelines for love. If love doesn't win now, wait. Perhaps it will win down the road for those who, like the father in the parable, go out until they see the wanderer who is still "a long way off."

If the facts of life seem to prove that, in some cases, love never wins and if you find yourself involved in a case so hopeless that you may as well give up loving, then *keep on loving*, no matter. For this is the way God loves, and it's the way we, therefore, ought to follow. Love doesn't have to win, because love is right. Even when love doesn't win, love is right.

And if love never wins in this lifetime, say to yourself that heaven can wait; faith never said that we must see results while we live. If that were so, some elements of eternity would be unnecessary.

Finally, in our own relationship to the Lord God, let us answer his love by loving him. He is the one who loves all his sons and daughters, even in their most unlovable times. So let us love him, this unparalleled Lover, in return. Thus, in some small measure we will help to prove that while love doesn't always win, in some of us it wins quite magnificently.

CHAPTER 7

Why Doesn't God Like Religious People?

LUKE 18:9-14: He also told this parable to some who trusted in themselves that they were righteous and regarded others with contempt: "Two men went up to the temple to pray, one a Pharisee and the other a tax collector. The Pharisee, standing by himself, was praying thus, 'God, I thank you that I am not like other people: thieves, rogues, adulterers, or even like this tax collector. I fast twice a week; I give a tenth of all my income.' But the tax collector, standing far off, would not even look up to heaven, but was beating his breast and saying, 'God, be merciful to me, a sinner!' I tell you, this man went down to his home justified rather than the other; for all who exalt themselves will be humbled, but all who humble themselves will be exalted."

J esus was a great teacher, partly because he was a great story-teller. We human beings love stories, because they take us out of our world even while they explain it to us. Effective stories teach us, usually without our knowing that they are doing so. Skilled teacher that he was, Jesus never concluded a story by saying, "Now here is the moral of the story." Sometimes the disciples—possessed by slowness of heart, like us—pressed him for an interpretation, but Jesus usually let the story stand on its own.

In so many instances, Jesus' parables came in response to a question. For all we know, perhaps all of them did. The gospel writers have grouped some of the parables in their respective books, such as in Matthew 13, but it's possible that Jesus told these stories at moments when someone said, "How is it, exactly, that the kingdom of God will come?" There were also instances when Jesus told a story because what he had to say was too sensitive to be said forthright. For that matter, some of it was difficult for his hearers to accept even when presented as a whimsical tale.

No doubt that was the case one day when Jesus suddenly said to all within earshot, "Let me tell you about these two men who went to the temple to pray." The people edged in closer to be sure they wouldn't miss a word. I can imagine one man grinning a little, because he's sure he's going to enjoy this story.

Jesus began, "One was a Pharisee and the other a tax collector." It's hard to pick heroes and villains from that cast. On the surface, of course, the people admired the Pharisees. They were in awe of their public righteousness, but they seldom liked them. It's hard to like someone who's always looking at you disapprovingly and perhaps even condescendingly. The tax collectors were no better. They were collaborating with a despised foreign government, that of the Romans. Not only were they collecting taxes—a burdensome calling at best—but also they were violating their ties with their own people and their own religious heritage each day they did so.

But the tax collectors did have one appealing virtue. It isn't one we like to mention, but it's there, all the same. They played a key role in the world of moral values by being someone everyone else could look down on. I suppose the whole world—even its most debased and criminal societies—has a moral pecking order. Everyone except the true saints looks for someone to whom he or she can point and say, "Hey, that one's worse than I am." The tax collectors played that role to perfection—and in so doing probably won the unconscious affection of the masses.

Back to the story. In the temple, the two men prayed. The Pharisee stood up for his prayer "and prayed about himself," as the New International Version puts it. When you read his prayer, you realize clearly that he was praying about himself.

"God, I thank thee that I am not like others," he said. Then he became specific. It is good to be specific in prayers, for it prevents lazy praying, or praying in generalities. But this kind of specificity wasn't very commendable. He began to list people he was glad he wasn't like: "Extortioners, the unjust, adulterers, or even like this tax collector." I suppose you could say he wasn't oblivious of other people in the world, he noticed them enough to be grateful that he was better than they were.

Having established his credentials negatively, by comparing himself with the common race of human creatures, he went to work on his positive record. "I fast twice a week, I give tithes of all that I get." It was an impressive record. Jewish law prescribed only one obligatory fast, on the Day of Atonement. But people who sought special merit also fasted on Mondays and Thursdays.

Unfortunately, this additional piety was probably tainted. The popular British writer and expositor William Barclay says that Monday and Thursday were the principal market days in Jerusalem, when the city was crowded with people. Those who fasted would often whiten their faces and dress in clothing that would mark them as being in pious mourning, thus drawing attention to themselves.

Meanwhile, in a far corner of the place of worship, the tax collector was praying. He wouldn't even lift his eyes to heaven. He was deeply agitated. He beat his clenched fists into his chest as he cried, "God, be merciful to me a sinner."

The crowd was enjoying the story. The two men had prayed just as the crowd might have expected they would. The Pharisee may not have been likeable, but it was true that he did everything he spoke of. Almost everyone in the crowd had seen his religious performances at one time or another. And while they didn't know what the tax collector would pray, they figured he had reason to stand off in a corner and weep about his sins. His cheating and lying were common knowledge; some in the crowd had been his victims. He had good reason to beat his breast and weep, and they were pleased to see him do so.

But Jesus' closing line shocked them. That isn't surprising, because his closing lines so often did just that. In this respect, the first-century crowds had an edge on us, because they were able to be shocked by Jesus' stories. We have domesticated them by familiarity to such an extent that we hardly recognize how shocking they are.

"I want to tell you," Jesus said, "that this tax collector went home justified. Right with God. The Pharisee didn't. And I'll tell you why. 'Everyone who makes himself great will be humbled, and everyone who humbles himself will be made great.'"

You and I like this story because we identify with the tax collector. We think of ourselves as the humble man who confessed he didn't deserve anything. We admire his humility, a virtue not easy to come by. True, he had plenty of reason to be humble, but, nevertheless, he was humble. As we read Jesus' commendation of the tax collector, we picture ourselves walking away from the temple in the same posture of quiet earnestness, humility pouring from every pore.

Unfortunately, we customarily read, teach, and preach this parable from the point of view of the tax collector. But when we view it from the painful vantage point of the Pharisee, we're closer to what Jesus originally intended. The gospel writer made that point quite clear by prefacing the parable with the explanation that Jesus "told this parable to some who trusted in themselves that they were righteous and despised others." It wasn't Jesus' aim to make the tax collectors feel better, but rather to stir the consciences of the Pharisees—all us Pharisees. Let's put ourselves, then, in his shoes.

On the one hand, it isn't easy. I don't really like the Pharisee. I've met him, and I don't like him. In fact, I've probably met almost everyone in his family, and they don't appeal to me, either. But on the other hand, you and I may resemble the Pharisee more than we like to admit, or than we even realize. I think, for instance, of that common phrase spoken by so many people in the midst of some difficult time: "Why me, Lord?" Let's face it: this is a Pharisee's question. The assumption here is that some other people (like this tax collector, Lord) perhaps deserve to suffer reversals, but I don't. If misfortune would come to them, we could understand it, because they have it coming to them. But *me?* Why me, Lord?

We're in a position to empathize with the Pharisee. We can understand him if he moves uneasily out on the edge of Jesus' crowd and asks himself, "Where have I gone wrong? Why doesn't God like me? And how could he possibly like the tax collector better than he likes me?" The truth is, most of us understand the Pharisee better than we want to. In some measure, we probably belong to his family. No, not many of us would be so audacious as to speak the words attributed to him in this parable, but most of us have entertained such words at some point in our private thoughts—perhaps even daily.

Consider the Pharisee's credentials for a moment. First, as he so painstakingly explained to God, he didn't commit any of the egregious, obvious sins. He wasn't dishonest, he wasn't unjust, and he wasn't an adulterer. You wouldn't be afraid to buy a used car from him, or to leave him alone in a room with your spouse. If he were your next-door neighbor, he might not be a barrel of laughs, but neither would he be a reason for worry. If everyone in the world were like the Pharisee, you could leave your doors unlocked at night and you wouldn't need a burglar alarm on your car.

Moreover, he was admirably religious. He tithed his income and he fasted twice a week. Quite honestly, in these things he was a better person than I am. I tithe my income and perhaps a bit more, but I don't fast twice a week. Come to think of it, I don't fast even once a week. You and I, who don't live with as much moral strictness and religious scrupulosity as the Pharisee, probably ought to be very careful about criticizing him, at least until we approximate more closely his level of conduct.

We might even say that the Pharisee had a spirit of gratitude. We may not like the way he showed it, but he had a certain thankfulness, nonetheless. "I thank you," he said to God, "that I am not like other people." Yes, that's a highly questionable kind of prayer, but we've heard expressions of gratitude from people today that have something of the same quality. And perhaps it's better than no gratitude at all.

You and I are so accustomed to seeing the Pharisee as the "heavy" in this little drama that it's almost impossible to put ourselves in his shoes. Worse yet, we don't recognize ourselves in him. It's probably true that most congregations in our Western world are made up of people who are close kin to the Pharisee. We are people who congratulate ourselves now and again on our moral achievement. We don't often do so in the temple, as the Pharisee did; perhaps we don't even belong to a congregation. We do so while reading the newspaper or while watching the evening news. Why can't all the world be like me, we say. If it were, there wouldn't be so many troubles. "I thank thee, Lord, that I pay my taxes. I curb my dog. I obey the speed limits. I don't burden society with drug use. I'm a contributor to society, not a problem. Why can't other people be like me?"

Don't we talk like that? And isn't that the Pharisee's prayer, even though we say it over the newspaper or at the business luncheon, rather than in the temple?

But why didn't God appreciate the Pharisee's goodness and religiosity? Or ours, when we are like him? For one thing, the

Pharisee was using religion to hold God at a distance. The purpose of religion, clearly, is to draw us nearer to God, and then to our fellow human beings. But the Pharisee was using religion to hold God at a safe distance, and other human beings at a level below. God wanted a place in the Pharisee's heart; the Pharisee wanted to give God a place in the ritual. God wanted truth and sincerity within; the Pharisee wanted a set of rules he could follow.

It's easy to get just enough religion to protect ourselves from God. The Pharisee should have known that, because he was a student of the scriptures. He knew, for example, that the prophet Amos had said, on behalf of God, "I hate and despise all your religious ceremonies and your solemn songs. . . . What I want from you is justice and righteousness."[1]

We like the kind of religion we can measure, because it protects us from more demanding issues. The Pharisee tithed—he gave a tenth of his income to church and charity. (I surely don't want to belittle tithing. I believe in it, practice it, and believe Christians ought to look upon it as the minimum in standards of giving. I regret that only a minority of professing Christians tithe, because even a Pharisee can do that much.) Tithing is manageable because it's measurable. All you have to do in order to tithe is to learn how to move the decimal point over one place when you receive your income. That's simple, isn't it? But God raises an issue that is terribly complex because it cannot be measured: Love me with all your heart, soul, mind, and strength. The Pharisee wisely answers, "I'd rather tithe." When we tithe, we know when we're done with our obligations, as we perceive them, whereas when we love, we're never really done.

So it is with fasting. Fasting is a good thing. I'm not an expert on the subject, but I've fasted from time to time and I've gleaned a small sense of its value. It is an act of devotion to God. But fasting is also measurable. If I give up a meal, or a day of food, or several days of food, I know what I've done. I can count it off by the calorie. But when God says, "Love your neighbor as yourself," I want to answer, "There is no end to that. It's an intangible commandment. It grows as I grow, so I never catch up with it."

True worship of God should make us humble, for it is in humility that we are more apt to love God and other people. The Pharisee's religion, however, made him proud. He had just enough religion to make him feel superior to other people. In many ways, he really was better than most people. But the point is that we don't have to be better than others. When we compare ourselves with other people, we almost always come out looking pretty good, unless we're the self-condemning sort. We're usually inclined, except in our gloomy moments, to see ourselves with a less critical eye and to be more conscious of our neighbor's faults than of his or her achievements. This is one point on which the Bible is so demanding. The Bible doesn't say, "You ought to be as good as the next person, and better than some"; it commands that we strive to be like God.

The Pharisee looked around him, probably a bit selectively, and saw how much better he was than other people—especially better than this tax collector. By the standards of his own time and religion, that wasn't saying much. Tax collectors were very low on the spiritual hit chart. Comparing himself with the tax collector was a little like a college graduate boasting that he or she knows more than a fourth grader. But he not only looked down on the tax collector, he also despised the tax collector. You can't make a case for loving God when you hate your brother or sister. In that regard, the Pharisee was in big trouble.

True religion makes us feel our need for God, so that we are drawn to him. Unfortunately, the Pharisee (as do a good many of us) had the kind of religion that makes one feel one can get along without God. Isn't that what the Pharisee had in mind in his prayer? He was saying, in effect, "How fortunate you are, Almighty, to have me!" The tax collector, on the other hand, was praying, "Do you see, O God, how badly I need you?"

Charles Clayton Morrison, perhaps the premier religious journalist of the early twentieth century, once said that the church is the only institution in the world whose membership is based on unworthiness to be a member. That's a fact that we have a hard time believing.

The great Episcopal leader Samuel Shoemaker often tried to make this point with his congregation at the Calvary Episcopal Church in Pittsburgh. A person must turn to God, he said one Sunday, "not as a gentleman in search of a religion but as a sinner in search of salvation." He noted that in the Anglican ritual a worshiper admits to God to being a "miserable offender" and that "there is no health in us." Then he became even more direct, insisting that the "respectable sinner" has no right to feel superior to someone whose sins "are merely disreputable when his own are absolutely disastrous."

Perhaps this statement in Dr. Shoemaker's sermon strikes a chord in each of us:

> The wickedest people I ever talked to are not the out-and-out pagan sinners, they are the people who have grown too good ever to be open to conviction of sin by the Holy Spirit, the people who believe that, on the whole, they are all right, the people who enjoy a good reputation, and live on the flattery of their neighbors. People like this can say their prayers a hundred times over, and confess their sins with all the unction in the world, and never become even dimly aware of sins that are the standing despair of the people who live under the same roof or work in the same office, with them.[2]

That's a tough statement. As an individual, I feel the sting of it; as a pastor for nearly forty years, I understand the passion with which Dr. Shoemaker spoke it. He was talking to all of us Pharisees. Particularly, he was confronting us with the damning danger Pharisees face: that they will shut themselves out of the grace of God.

The root problem for good people is not simply that they have a holier-than-thou attitude, it is that they are possessed by a holier-than-God attitude. They condemn in judgment those whom God does not, and they refuse to give room to the grace of God, not only for others but also for themselves. For others, because they don't believe they deserve it; for themselves, because they don't believe they need it.

The heart of the matter isn't that God doesn't like good people, it is that *good people don't like God.* They will not allow themselves to understand or to accept the quality in God's nature that stands out above all others: *grace,* as we know it in the New Testament, and mercy or lovingkindness *(hesedh)* as it is described in the Hebrew scriptures.

Most of us are more in danger of the sins of the Pharisee than those of the tax collector. We can probably say that we aren't guilty of too many heinous sins. But quite possibly that's because, as one anonymous social critic has said, "Nothing makes it easier to resist temptation than a proper upbringing, a sound set of values, and witnesses." Many of us have been kept from trouble by "witnesses." We've been free of the more glaring sins, not because they were unattractive to us, but because we were afraid of the social, legal, or physical consequences.

Before we leave this parable, we ought to introduce another character. This one never appears yet dominates the story. If our medieval ancestors ever cast this story as a morality play, they must have made this character the villain: Pride.

Pride is such a subtle devil because it is, at first, a hero. In proper guise, pride is an essential element in our human personalities. When a person is converted, part of the transformation is a restoration of the sense of dignity and self-worth; that is, of pride.

But pride can change costumes before our very eyes, so that the first aid becomes the chief villain. And pride so quickly comes to work in the good person. Having won some battle of the soul, whether small or large, we easily conclude that we are now better than others.

Perhaps Cain was the first Pharisee. When God approved of Abel's sacrifice more than Cain's, Cain's pride was hurt. How could God show such poor taste, by preferring Abel's offering to his own? Worse yet, pride kept Cain from making things right. God graciously held out the opportunity for him to repent and try again. But pride makes it impossible for us to repent, because repentance requires us to acknowledge that we have been wrong. Pride also makes it difficult for us to accept grace, because grace is humbling; pride would rather do it alone.

In the aforementioned sermon by Dr. Shoemaker, he noted that our characteristic sins (the sins that especially characterize good people)—impatience, irritability, self-indulgence—have behind them the "ever-present spectre of pride." They are, Shoemaker said, "just a front for pride."

G. K. Chesterton chose often to use his mystery-novel alter ego Father Brown as spokesperson for his deepest convictions. In one instance Father Brown observed that no one is really any good until he knows "how bad he is, or might be . . . till he's squeezed out of his soul the last drop of the oil of the Pharisees."[3]

That's terribly difficult for good people, however, because we are so rarely confronted with our sins. Jeffrey Lynn Speller, a special lecturer at Harvard University, says that upper-income people and executives are often surrounded by a conspiracy of silence. Family members are made silent by a vested interest in the person's prestige and income. Close subordinates fear they might lose their jobs if the person were fired. Even colleagues are silent because they fear the company might suffer great losses if important players learned that high-level executives were dysfunctional. Worse yet, nobody really monitors such a person's performance.[4]

Good, moral people—including both lay and professional church leaders—are in the same situation. A pastor hesitates to speak candidly to the person everyone looks up to, and lay people are equally hesitant to approach a pastor. As for bishops and other church officials, even the angels and archangels may refuse the assignment. So the villain, Pride, works on, unchecked.

Perhaps that's what Martin Luther had in mind when he called repentance a life task. Maybe he was warning us that when we become good, we need more than ever to be experts in repentance, lest we lose our souls. And perhaps that's the passion in Elizabeth Barrett Browning's cry in *Aurora Leigh*, when she lists all the ways good people can, self-blinded, do evil, and then appeals,

> Now may the good God pardon all good men!

To which this Pharisee would say: *Amen.*

CHAPTER 8

Pardon My Insistence

MATTHEW 22:1-10: Once more Jesus spoke to them in parables, saying: "The kingdom of heaven may be compared to a king who gave a wedding banquet for his son. He sent his slaves to call those who had been invited to the wedding banquet, but they would not come. Again he sent other slaves, saying, 'Tell those who have been invited: Look, I have prepared my dinner, my oxen and my fat calves have been slaughtered, and everything is ready; come to the wedding banquet.' But they made light of it and went away, one to his farm, another to his business, while the rest seized his slaves, mistreated them, and killed them. The king was enraged. He sent his troops, destroyed those murderers, and burned their city. Then he said to his slaves, 'The wedding is ready, but those invited were not worthy. Go therefore into the main streets, and invite everyone you find to the wedding banquet.' Those slaves went out into the streets and gathered all whom they found, both good and bad; so the wedding hall was filled with guests."

T he people who opposed Jesus couldn't find many things about him to criticize. After all, it's hard to say something bad about a person who goes about doing good, helping the poor and healing the sick, and all of it for nothing. But there was one thing they pounced on: He went to so many parties, they said, and furthermore, he usually went with the wrong people.

It was a fair observation on their part, even if the implication was unfair, because it's certainly true that Jesus often talked about parties. Parties were factors in a number of his parables.

One story Jesus told was based entirely on a party. The kingdom of heaven, Jesus said, can be compared to a king who gave a marriage

69

feast for his son. Sounds like a happy story, right? Well, not necessarily. As the time of the party drew near, the king sent out servants in the custom of the times to call those who had been invited. With extraordinary discourtesy, those invited refused to come. (At this point you and I say to ourselves, How could people respond this way to an invitation from their king? Clearly, Jesus intends in very dramatic ways for us to realize just how unthinkable is our human response to God's generosity.)

So the king sent other servants, perhaps ones he felt would be more convincing. They were to tell the invited guests that the oxen and the fat calves were killed and that everything was ready. This would add both excitement and urgency to the invitation. "The food's on the table. Hurry!" But the people made light of the renewed invitation. They offered ridiculous excuses, which simply indicated that they felt they had better things to do than to come to the wedding party for the king's son. Some of them, irrationally, even became brutal. Not content to reject the invitation, they seized the servants, mistreated and shamed them, and even killed some of them.

Now the king was angry. He ordered his troops to destroy the murderers and to burn their city. But that didn't solve the problem of his party. It would still be bitterly disappointing to have no one at such a festive occasion. So he said to his servants, "The feast is ready, but the people I originally invited were undeserving. Now go to the main streets and invite as many people as you find."

So the servants did just that. They went everywhere, to safe streets and unsafe streets, and found people both bad and good—an astonishingly nondescript crowd—and invited them in. Soon the wedding hall was filled with people, and the king was able to have a celebration properly honoring his son's wedding.

This strange and somewhat delightful story had two obvious interpretations. First, Jesus was telling the crowd that God had originally invited to the heavenly kingdom a chosen people, the Jews, and that they had refused. Not only did they offer unworthy excuses, but they also persecuted and killed the king's messengers, the prophets. Since those originally invited wouldn't accept God's grand invitation, he finally sent messengers out into the world's unlikely highways, where they invited everyone, including Gentiles. This is clearly the primary interpretation of the parable.

The secondary interpretation is one we can make personally. Our Lord has prepared a great celebration, the grand homecoming of heaven and eternity. He has invited everyone to come to this greatest-of-all celebrations. But like the people in the parable, many of us refuse the invitation with absurd excuses. We give more attention to the passing, relatively inconsequential matters of life than to an opportunity to come to the King's feast. And sometimes, as we look at those who are coming, it seems that many unlikely people are on their way to God's great day—people we might have thought unworthy.

Many scholars say that the primary focus of the parable is the event itself, rather than the invited guests or the king. The parable could be rightly titled "The Great Banquet." I find myself fascinated, however, by a minor figure, an unnamed servant. I try to imagine his feelings during the helter-skelter events of this story.

How did he feel, for instance, when his master's original invitation was received with so much disdain? Was he crushed that people could be so indifferent to an invitation from the king? Did he want to forget his servant role and shake some of the potential guests, saying, "Don't you realize who it is that's inviting you? Can't you see how much of an honor is being extended in an invitation to share with the king in the marriage of his son?"

Imagine a young Christian who is infused with the lovely, somewhat bumbling enthusiasm of one who has just been overwhelmed by the grace of God. She can't wait to share the Good News with someone she loves. "The most wonderful thing has happened. You know how confused I used to be, how I didn't know what was worth living for? Well, now I've found what I was looking for. Let me tell you about it." But to her surprise, the good friend is indifferent. In the parable, the invited guests "went away, one to his farm, another to his business." So it is that her friends respond to her. "Religion is nice for those who have time for it. We think it's very appealing that you've become so enthusiastic. A little quaint, though. Almost offensive at times. But we don't mind your excitement if you just keep it to yourself. Meanwhile, we have more important things to do. Have you noticed what's happening on the stock market these days?"

Likewise, the servant wonders why the people cannot see that nothing compares with an invitation from the king. He even wonders if he has somehow done a poor job of delivering the invitation. If only he could convey the wonder of the invitation, which now so thrills his life!

As the story moves along, the servant's confusion increases as he is given new instructions. When Luke recounts the parable in his Gospel, he has the king say, "Go out quickly to the streets and lanes of the city, and bring in the poor and maimed and blind and lame." This is an element of the story that Luke, who so much loved the least and the lost, would be sure to emphasize.

A title by the English cleric and poet G. A. Studdert-Kennedy asks "Why Aren't All the Best Chaps Christians?" Why, indeed, do people who seem such likely candidates for the Kingdom turn an indifferent ear? And why do we so often see more earnest and passionate responses from unlikely souls? Perhaps it is because the people we deem most appropriate are too wrapped up in their own affairs—their farms and their stores, to say nothing of their concerts and golf matches.

The dramatic American poet Vachel Lindsay described General William Booth, founder of the Salvation Army, entering heaven. Booth was surely a servant who went into the highways and byways of life to bring in every imaginable human being. Lindsay described the procession this way:

> Walking lepers followed, rank on rank,
> Lurching bravos from the ditches dank,
> Drabs from the alleyways and drug fiends pale—
> Minds still passion-ridden, soul-powers frail:—
> Vermin-eaten saints with moldy breath,
> Unwashed legions with the ways of Death—[1]

That sounds very much like the crowd the king suggested bringing in, as Luke reports it. Jesus' audience would have understood this part of the parable better than we do, because they believed so much in charity and because they felt there should be no waste. Nevertheless, it's an unlikely scene: a wedding feast for the king's son attended by "unwashed legions with the ways of Death." It isn't the kind of party you'd expect a king to have.

I wonder how the servant felt about all of this. We read that he and his associates "gathered all the people they could find, good and bad alike." But surely he was perplexed by the king's instructions. Perhaps he felt like the French queen who, after hearing from her court chaplain that God cared for the poor and rejected, expressed the opinion that his God had very strange taste. Sometimes we feel that way, too, don't we?

This was the sort of question that troubled the good people of Jesus' time. They were sincerely uncomfortable that Jesus, who was so clearly a good person himself and who gave evidence in so many ways that the Spirit of God was on him, could nevertheless choose to associate with people who lived on the edges of life. In a measure, this parable may have been addressed to the good people; perhaps Jesus was saying, "You didn't accept me, so now it's the less reputable elements to whom I go."

I wonder, too, if the servant lost sight of the fact that he was inviting people to a party. When your invitation is being rejected on all sides, you may begin to lose faith in the party. You wonder, If it's a party, then how come nobody is excited about attending?

And after the city which so badly rejected the king was destroyed, I wonder if desperation became the dominant tone in the servant's appeal on his next round of invitations. Did he stop saying, "Come to the king's party. We're going to have good food, good fun, lots of dancing"—and say instead, "Between you and me, you'd better accept this invitation, or what happened to the folks in the city will happen to you, too"?

If you and I have come to know Jesus Christ as Lord and Savior and if we have found joy in following him, we should find it easy to remember that we're inviting people to a *party*. Helmut Thielicke, the great German preacher and professor, put it perfectly: "Repentance and remorse always come soon enough, but joy can never come too soon. We who know Jesus Christ have only to proclaim joy."[2] Thielicke rightly insists that there must be something festive and happy about our whole Christian manner, or people will not believe that we are messengers of the king.

William Barclay chose the New Testament Greek word *kalos* as the most descriptive word for what characterizes Christian personality at its best. He suggests that it should be translated *winsome*, for while the words *good* and *beautiful* are usually used, these words fail to catch the quality of attractiveness the Greek word implies. It is this winsomeness which should mark the servant as he or she goes out into the highways to invite people to the feast. There ought to be something about the servant's style that gives one a foretaste of the warmth that lies ahead in the wedding feast.

This may be the particular attractiveness, if only at a superficial level, of some television ministries. They often seem to convey a festive feeling, as if they are announcing a party. For whatever it's worth, they profess joy in their faith. That's appealing to people who have the impression that religion is just one step removed from a root canal.

This doesn't mean that Christianity is a cheap fix. Jesus invited us to take up our crosses and follow him, and any Christian who is without a cross is not only shallow but fraudulent. Nevertheless, when Jesus spoke of a yoke, he affirmed that his yoke is easy and his burden light. He warned his disciples that they might lose home and families by following him, but he also promised that they would be rewarded many fold. He also said that he had come to give us life, abundant life. Likewise, when the apostle Paul wrote to one of the early congregations about the nature of the Christian life, he put the issue of joy in a memorable figure of speech. "Do not get drunk with wine," he said, "which will only ruin you; instead, be filled with the Spirit."[3]

That's party talk—party talk in the style of an invitation to a wedding feast. It reminds us again that the Christian life is not, by biblical definition, a tedious affair. Demanding, yes, but tedious and tasteless, no. By definition, the Christian life has a quality of exuberance. The servant who invites others to the continuing party needs to remember that and to demonstrate it by his or her style.

Yet with all of that, the servant was told to be insistent. My tables still aren't full, the king said, so go out into the highways and byways and *compel* people to come in. That's a hard saying for me, because I'm not the salesperson type. I tried several times to sell encyclopedia sets. I thought I could do it, because I love books and learning; but I found it hard to be that aggressive. The truth is, I hesitate to ask a server for a second glass of iced tea. I'm not naturally an insistent servant.

I find it easier to be insistent, however, when I remember that I'm inviting people to a party. I can't explain everything about heaven and hell, but there are some matters of which I am very sure. I know that I've been invited to a party. I remember when I first responded to Christ's invitation, as a sixth grader of limited understanding but of unspoiled hunger. I was not a drug addict or an enemy of society; to the contrary, I was a better-than-average student who knew little about dire sins except as I overheard adult conversations. Nevertheless, the invitation seemed to come to me with particular urgency. I wonder why, as I look back. How could my alienation from God have seemed so pressing, when my rebellion was still so unformed? No matter; I know only that the invitation was urgent—and the memory is vivid still, even looking back over more than half a century—that I resisted it during the singing of an extended invitation hymn, that eventually I accepted, and that with my acceptance, I experienced peculiar joy.

I know also that in the years which have followed, I have enjoyed many benefits of the party. Even on my poorest days I hear the music of the Party, off in the distance. It is that lovely, warmly haunting music which stirs me to keep my life and thoughts in order. For if the music heard from a distance is so enchanting, then how wonderful, indeed, will the ultimate Party be! And it is when this sense is strongest that I am the most effective, the most insistent servant.

When C. S. Lewis titled his spiritual autobiography *Surprised by Joy*, he acknowledged that what he had sought most in life was that almost indescribable quality, *joy*. Lewis notes that as he uses the word, it is "a technical term and must be sharply distinguished both from Happiness and from Pleasure." He disputes the idea that anyone who has tasted it "would ever, if both were in his power, exchange it for all the pleasures in the world."[4] He notes at a later point that joy is not a substitute for sex but that sex is very often a substitute for joy, and then challenges, "I sometimes wonder whether all pleasures are not substitutes for Joy."[5]

Yet as he comes to the end of his story, Lewis observes that the subject (joy) "has lost nearly all interest for me since I became a Christian." Why? He answers, because "it was valuable only as a pointer to something other and outer."[6]

Perhaps that's the issue of this parable and those others which speak of the kingdom of heaven as a party or a celebration, as so many do. When we are invited to a party, we are drawn by the appeal of the excitement; but when we arrive, the fulfillment comes in visiting with the dear friend who is there, or in a conversation in which the human soul is made to feel complete. When that happens, we don't think much about the taste of the *hors d'oeuvres* or the elegance of the centerpiece. A person may be brought to Christian commitment by the attractiveness of heaven or the fear of hell, but people who mature in Christian experience find their highest fulfillment in their communion with God.

The longing for joy may well be one of the most, if not the most, compelling of reasons for our quest for God. Perhaps this longing is the essence of the soul's restlessness to which Augustine referred or maybe it is the God-shaped void of Pascal. As such, it is a prime reason for the inviting servant to be insistent. What a privilege to be able to offer someone an invitation to the party for which they have always instinctively longed! How can we help being insistent when we carry such an invitation?

So if you have a good friend, someone for whom you really care, invite him or her to the Party. And if you have a son or a daughter, a parent or a sibling or a spouse, hurry with the invitation. The king said to the servant, "Compel them!" Say to them, "Don't miss the party!"

It's the one Event in all of time and eternity that we dare not miss. Of course we would be insistent! How could we be otherwise?

CHAPTER **9**

The Prodigal Who Stayed at Home

LUKE 15:25-32: "Now his elder son was in the field; and when he came and approached the house, he heard music and dancing. He called one of the slaves and asked what was going on. He replied, 'Your brother has come, and your father has killed the fatted calf, because he has got him back safe and sound.' Then he became angry and refused to go in. His father came out and began to plead with him. But he answered his father, 'Listen! For all these years I have been working like a slave for you, and I have never disobeyed your command; yet you have never given me even a young goat so that I might celebrate with my friends. But when this son of yours came back, who has devoured your property with prostitutes, you killed the fatted calf for him!' Then the father said to him, 'Son, you are always with me, and all that is mine is yours. But we had to celebrate and rejoice, because this brother of yours was dead and has come to life; he was lost and has been found.'"

*I*f all the chapters in this book were like this one, the book would be more correctly titled "Parables from the Neglected Side." It seems clear that the parable of the prodigal son was intended to have the focus we shall now consider. We have been so captured by the sentiment, warmth, and emotion of the story of the younger son, his wanderings and the love with which he was accepted on his return, that we have missed what Jesus was raising as the crucial point: How will the older brothers of the world, the conventionally religious, respond to the grace of God, both as it is experienced by others who enjoy its benefits, and as it is offered to them?

In other words, the focal point of this story is not the younger brother but the older one. The younger one generally appeals to us more because of the dramatic quality of his story. But the story does not reach its climax in his return or in the celebration that followed; rather, its climax is in the way the older brother responded to these events. When read that way—the way it appears in the scriptures—the story doesn't end satisfactorily, because there is, in fact, no conclusion. The conclusion is left up to the hearers. Most of the time we take the open-endedness of the parables for granted, but we seem to miss the conclusion of this story. For all practical purposes, we stop reading before the story is over, probably because we are so happy with the younger son's homecoming.

Familiar as it is, hear the story once more. A certain man had two sons. One day the younger son, having grown restless, asked his father if he might collect his inheritance early. We should note at this point that both sons got their share; the father "divided his property between them."[1] This meant the younger son received one-third and the older son received two-thirds, although probably the older held his share in conjunction with his father.

Soon after the younger man got his share, he headed off to a far country. There he was caught up in wild, self-destructive living so that before long he had lost all his money. He was reduced to feeding swine in order to stay alive.

But one day, in his despair, he came to his senses. He realized that even the servants in his father's house lived better than he was living, so he decided to return home. When he was still a long way off, his father saw him and ran to welcome him. He not only restored him to his place in the household, but he also threw a grand homecoming party to celebrate his return.

The party featured a calf that had been fattened, ready for just this occasion. But when the party was at its height, with happiness flowing freely and laughter filling the hall, the older brother came in from the field. He had been working late, as he so often did. He was an industrious person, eager to use his time well, and probably eager to increase his holdings. Now, weary at the end of a strenuous day, he heard the unfamiliar sounds of partying. Then he learned the reason: His no-good brother had returned, and his father was having a celebration.

The older brother wouldn't go in to the party. His father left the fun-making and feasting to plead with him to come in, but the brother wouldn't be moved. "Look," he said, "I've worked my fingers to the bone for you and for this farm all these years, and you've never done anything for me. I couldn't even have a dinner featuring a goat. Then this son of yours comes home—this fellow who has wasted his inheritance on prostitutes—and you kill that little prize calf for him. You bet your life I'm not going in to that party!"

The father answered, "My son, you are always with me. Everything I have is yours. But it's time for a party, because this brother of yours was dead and now he's alive again. He was lost and now he's found."

And that's where the story ends. Clearly enough, Jesus left it to the crowd to write the conclusion. That's evident from the way this whole wonderful chapter begins. We are told at the outset that the tax collectors and sinners were gathered around Jesus—as they so often were—to hear him. Theoretically, that should have made the religious leaders happy, to see such a vital interest in religion. But it didn't. "The Pharisees and the teachers of the law muttered, 'This man welcomes sinners and eats with them.'"[2] The "good people" couldn't understand why Jesus was so pleased to associate with sinners. It was at this point that Jesus told the three stories of the lost coin, the lost sheep, and the family sorrow. All said the same thing: Don't hate what is lost; rather, rejoice in its being found. The climax of the stories is in the apparent anticlimax with which the third story ends, the portion we generally seem to overlook, the encounter between the older brother and his father. Herein is the point.

Here Jesus introduced the "good people" to themselves, to the older brother inside them. They were the people who stood at the edge of the crowd when Jesus was celebrating with the prodigals. And Jesus ended his story without telling them what the older brother did, because *they* were going to have to decide, since they were the older brother. Luke never tells us how this altar call turned out.

We are usually so fascinated with the wonderful stories of the lost sheep, the lost coin, and the prodigal son that we miss the point Jesus wanted most to make: What happens to the older brother? That's a prime question for most of us, because many of us are like this older brother. We live quite responsible lives, obey the basic laws, are generally moral, and probably work hard. We especially work hard out in the father's fields—community projects, PTA, service clubs, voter registration drives, half-a-hundred church committees. We're in a position to sympathize with the older brother. We understand him. It may be that we've even said at times that we don't blame him for being angry. He had good reason to complain.

Jesus loved this older brother, to be sure. At no point does he speak harshly of him. But it's also clear that Jesus was disappointed in him. There is something very wrong with this older brother, but what is it?

First, the older brother seemed to envy the sinner. There was more to his envy than the party which celebrated his brother's homecoming. His refusal to attend the party might have been mean-spirited, but it does not reveal hidden depths of weakness. I fear he may have envied his brother for more reasons than just the party. He's the one, you recall, who tells us that his brother spent his money on prostitutes; there is nothing about prostitutes in the story until the older brother mentions them. Perhaps he was recalling village gossip, because, without a doubt, that's the sort of rumor which most often has spread through the neighborhood. Obviously he hadn't got the word firsthand from his brother, because he hadn't yet seen his brother—he didn't even know his brother had returned.

Judging from what I know of human nature, the prostitute idea was something he conjured up in his very human, somewhat lustful mind. He probably said to himself often, before his brother's return, "I know what he's doing there in the city. He's spending his time with beautiful, wicked women. Rotten dog!" Then, under his breath, "Lucky dog!"

Good people are sometimes like that. We do right things, but we long for bad things. In one of his poems, Charles Wesley thanks God that as a young man he escaped the more grievous sins; he was not, he said, one of the "young corrupters." But he confesses that it was because of his "sacred cowardice." That is, he knew that it was not his goodness which had kept him from sin, but the fear of the consequences. Many of us might rightly acknowledge that we are in the same category. We would get in much more trouble if it weren't for our fear of public opinion, or if we weren't so anxious to protect our standing in the community.

Sometimes when "good people" express their horror at the conduct of another, it seems they are savoring the details. When they say, "Isn't that shameful? Can you imagine someone doing a thing like that?" there is a strong suggestion they may at the moment be salivating with envy. The older brother was like that. He envied his younger brother. To all appearances, he was a moral man, industrious and thrifty. But in his heart it may have been a far different matter.

The older brother had never really discovered the joys of home; no more, perhaps, than the younger brother before his days of wandering. He didn't realize how fortunate he was to be here, living in the daily blessing of a loving father. No wonder, then, that he asked his father, "What have you ever given me?" The people who listened as Jesus told the story knew what the father had given him, because the law of the culture required that the older brother get two-thirds of the family property at the time of distribution. He had done very well! He had the prestige, the comfort, and the challenge of a successful family operation. More important, he had the privilege of working with his father, someone who obviously loved deeply and generously. Even with all of that, he looked at his father and asked, "What have you given me?" He needed what his brother experienced in the pig pen: to "come to himself."

Frankly, it is easier to have such a personality awakening in one of life's pig pens than in our undisturbed routine. If we can live in the midst of goodness and not recognize its quality at least to a measure, then goodness hasn't made much of an impression on us. When we are surrounded by blessings and don't know we're blessed, we are pretty poor. We might as well not be blessed at all. Such was the state of this older son.

So it was with many of the religious people of Jesus' day. They were scrupulous in following the details of their religion, but they weren't enjoying it. They were working hard at the business of religion, but without fulfillment or lift. Then when they saw rank sinners coming to Jesus and enjoying the faith and friendship they found in him, they were bewildered. In fact, they resented it. They had lived in the house of religion all their lives, but had never experienced the joy of being there. Do you know anyone like that?

It's obvious that the younger son was wasting himself. He did it conspicuously and dramatically, in drunken parties and in settings where he could call out, "I'll buy drinks for everyone here!" It was easy to see that he was wasting his life away because he was doing so with a flourish. And, of course, it was easy to see how such a life would turn out. There came a time when he was threadbare, dirty, hungry, feeding pigs, and wishing he could eat as well as the pigs did. It was easy to see how the younger brother wasted himself and what came of it.

But the older brother was wasting his life away, too—not as obviously or dramatically as the younger brother, but just as harmfully and, ultimately, just as tragically. While the younger brother wasted himself in crude, riotous living, the older one did so in mean, small, selfish living.

I have worked in rescue missions where I've seen how pathetically a human being can throw his or her life away, but I've also had the same feeling in tasteful, middle-class and upper middle-class homes. Is it really any more of a waste for an alcoholic to spend all he or she has on liquor than for a buy-a-holic to purchase hundreds of pairs of shoes or scores of pairs of slacks? Of course, someone answers; first, because the person who buys inordinate amounts of clothing can afford it, and second, because such buying won't put a person on Skid Row or into a drug treatment center. True; but it's a matter of values. I think the deterioration of soul that comes when we become absorbed with material things is as serious an illness as drug addiction—perhaps worse, in that it isn't easily recognized and therefore goes untreated. I doubt that anyone's spirit or character can afford profligate spending. Materialism, too, is an intoxication.

When we hear of persons who burn out their brains with drugs, we mourn the waste of human resources. But the waste is just as great if all we do with our brains is make money or feed the ego. If we don't do something of worth with our lives and our money, we've come to live in our own kind of skid row. Perhaps that's why some people in comfortable circumstances feel so unfulfilled and so disappointed in life.

One more word about the older brother, and perhaps it's the worst of all: *He didn't know his father.* He had grown up under his father's kindness and love, yet somehow he never seemed to understand him. You can see this tragic flaw in the conversation about the younger son. The older brother couldn't see how his father could love the boy, or why he would want to celebrate his return. He called the other boy "your son," while the father tried to remind him that he was his brother. But he couldn't acknowledge he had a brother, because he didn't understand his father's heart.

Sybil Canon recalls an experience from her teenage years reminiscent of the older brother. Her Uncle Chester was an alcoholic; in fact, in their small Mississippi town he was known as the town drunk. When Sybil was fifteen, Uncle Chester and Aunt Mattie came to live with her, and though Sybil had become a Christian as a small girl and had shortly thereafter dedicated herself to Christian service, and although she was already the president of the youth group in her church, she could hardly bear the sight of her uncle, let alone treat him kindly.

Uncle Chester came to a revival service where Sybil was the soloist. When the evangelist asked those who were Christians to stand, Sybil proudly did so. The next morning as Uncle Chester fried the breakfast bacon, he said, "Some people at church last night misunderstood the preacher's directions. He asked for all the Christians to stand, and a lot of people who *aren't* Christians stood up, too."

Sybil knew his quiet comment was aimed at her, and it called forth all her bitter resentment. "Do you dare doubt my Christianity?" she screamed. "Your wife has to support you, and everybody in Iuka laughs at you. You can't walk straight! You can't talk without slurring and slobbering, and you smell like a gutter. I can't stand having you in my mother's house. I can't stand seeing Aunt Mattie put up with you. The truth is, I can't stand *you!* Do you know what you are, Uncle Chester? You're a drunk, a worthless drunk!"

Chester didn't look up from his frying pan, but he answered quietly, "Sybil, I know what I am, but do you know what you are?" That's probably the hardest of all questions for the older brother to face. It's so very difficult for an "older brother" to see himself or herself for what he or she may be. In any event, Sybil Canon remembers this as the question that changed her life. She realized that with all her claims to Christianity and her parading of her religion, she had never shown Christian love to her Uncle Chester.

After school that day she rushed home to find her uncle and to ask for his forgiveness. They went to church together that evening, and Sybil walked down the aisle again, this time to confess to the congregation that she had been a Pharisee, confident of her own spirituality without really seeing herself very clearly.[3]

The poor older brother didn't know his father. I have a feeling that there may have been servants in the household who understood the father's heart better than did his elder son.

How is it possible to live in such proximity to goodness and never come to appreciate it nor want to emulate it? The best goodness is marked by winsomeness; I'm sure the father in the parable had such a quality. But most of us know, either by experience in our own lives or by observing others, that one can be surrounded by beauty yet never really make it one's own. The father was a giving, loving, caring human being, but the older brother never seemed to grasp it. He didn't see his father's love as it was expressed to him, and he didn't want it expressed to his younger brother.

That's why I call this older brother (as others must have done before me) "the prodigal who stayed at home." He never went to the city and never, as far as we know, spent his money in riotous living; but he was a prodigal. In his heart, he envied the younger brother, he never discovered the joys of home, he wasted himself as badly (even though not as conspicuously) as the younger brother did, and he never understood his father. How could one be more prodigal than that?

Someone once asked the preacher Friedrich Krummacher who the older brother was. Krummacher answered, "I learned it only yesterday. *Myself.*"[4] There's a chance the same thing might be said of you and me. Growing up respectable, moral, and religious, we may in truth be just as prodigal—just as far from home—as if we had gone to the far country of corruption.

If so, I have good news for us. The Father will welcome us home. He'll have a party for us, too. "Everything I have is yours," he'll say. "Come in and join the party. Better yet: Come in and make it a party!"

CHAPTER 10

A Case for the Un-hired Hand

MATTHEW 20:1-15: "For the kingdom of heaven is like a landowner who went out early in the morning to hire laborers for his vineyard. After agreeing with the laborers for the usual daily wage, he sent them into his vineyard. When he went out about nine o'clock, he saw others standing idle in the marketplace; and he said to them, 'You also go into the vineyard, and I will pay you whatever is right.' So they went. When he went out again about noon and about three o'clock, he did the same. And about five o'clock he went out and found others standing around; and he said to them, 'Why are you standing here idle all day?' They said to him, 'Because no one has hired us.' He said to them, 'You also go into the vineyard.' When evening came, the owner of the vineyard said to his manager, 'Call the laborers and give them their pay, beginning with the last and then going to the first.' When those hired about five o'clock came, each of them received the usual daily wage. Now when the first came, they thought they would receive more; but each of them also received the usual daily wage. And when they received it, they grumbled against the landowner, saying, 'These last worked only one hour, and you have made them equal to us who have borne the burden of the day and the scorching heat.' But he replied to one of them, 'Friend, I am doing you no wrong; did you not agree with me for the usual daily wage? Take what belongs to you and go; I choose to give to this last the same as I give to you. Am I not allowed to do what I choose with what belongs to me? Or are you envious because I am generous?'"

W hen we speak of Jesus as the Great Teacher, we probably get a wrong image in our minds. Unconsciously we imagine him in a modern classroom, with students sitting in orderly rows. His teaching took place in a quite different forum. His classroom was a roadway or a marketplace—almost anywhere people might be found, and almost always out of doors. In many cases he probably taught as he walked. Frequently he was seeking to get and hold the attention of people who were themselves on the run—shopping, tending errands, going about the business of the day. If he were to reach them, he must capture their attention quickly and hold it in spite of distractions.

That's why the parables were such a masterful teaching device. They were a little like soap operas in their ability to make an immediate claim on attention and in their focus on the common elements of life, which would be of immediate interest to almost everyone.

Often the parables came as answers to questions from the crowd, sometimes from belligerent individuals and sometimes from souls on the search for faith. So it was that a rich young man one day sought out Jesus to ask how he might inherit eternal life. Jesus answered his question carefully, which meant that he led him at last to the issue of his wealth and of the sacrifices he would have to make if he were to follow God.

The young man left in sorrow, because he wasn't ready to make such a demanding decision. As he left, the disciples began to raise questions. It troubled them that a man who was in so many ways such an attractive candidate for eternal life would nevertheless reject it. They probably felt, as many of us do, that someone who had such wealth must be a better-than-average prospect for God. Besides, he was apparently so sincere. In the midst of the discussion, Peter raised a question probably on the minds of all the disciples but which only Peter would be audacious enough to ask: "Master, we've left everything to follow you. What will we get in return?"

Jesus explained that in the day of judgment, all who have made great sacrifices for him will be rewarded a hundred times over, and that in addition they will inherit eternal life. Then he added, "But many who are first will be last, and many who are last will be first."[1] And with that somewhat enigmatic statement, Jesus launched into this story.

A landowner went into the marketplace early in the morning to hire some day laborers to work in his vineyard. We assume it was harvest time, which meant additional help was urgently needed. The man agreed to pay these workers the standard rate, a silver piece for a day's work. The laborers were happy to get a job, and happy to accept the usual arrangement.

Some three hours later, at around nine o'clock in the morning, the owner returned to the market and found other men waiting for employment. He hired them, too, but this time he didn't agree on a specific sum. He said simply, "I will pay you whatever is right." Again at noon and at three in the afternoon, he followed the same procedure.

Now the day was nearly over. I imagine the farmer was extremely anxious to finish the harvest that very day. Perhaps the weather was threatening, or perhaps the grapes were at their peak for wine-making. In any event, at five o'clock, with only an hour of working time remaining, he went again to the marketplace and found some potential workers still waiting there. When you stop to think of it, there is something quite sad about workers who are still looking for a job at five o'clock of an afternoon when the workday ends at six. But there is something suspicious, too. The farmer wondered: "Why have you been standing here all day long doing nothing?" They answered, "Because no one has hired us."[2]

So the landowner hired them. Hardly an hour later, he asked his foreman to call the workers in so that they might be paid. For some reason he began payment—illogically, it seems—with those who had been hired last, only an hour before. Perhaps he wanted to see their surprise and delight upon receiving a silver piece, a full day's wages for only an hour's work. So it went down the line, for those who had worked only portions of the day.

Those who had been part of the first crew to be hired watched the proceedings with growing anticipation. If this landowner had so much money that he would pay a day's wages for an hour's work, or if he were simply so careless of money, well, then, what might he do for those who had done him the most good?

But they were soon disappointed. When they received their pay, it was just what they had been promised—a piece of silver—and just what the farmer had given those latecomers who had worked only an hour. They began to grumble, and with good reason. "We've borne the burden and the heat of the day," they said. "These other fellows are Johnny-come-latelies, yet they get as much as we do. It's not fair."

The landowner answered, "What do you mean, not fair? How much did I promise you? A silver piece, right? And how much did I give you? Just what I promised. Now if I want to be generous, that's my business. After all, it's my money."

As you well know, Jesus was not developing a new manual for employer-employee relations. Nor was he giving us a system of economics. He was trying to instruct his disciples, and you and me, about what God and heaven are like, and the result was a dramatic expression of grace. As teacher Richard Meadows points out, the rule of the business world is that the last hired is the first fired, while grace declares that the last hired is the first paid. There's a certain loving logic in this, for these last-hired need more kindness, since they've known fewer benefits.

But Peter and the other apostles didn't like the story. Peter had reminded Jesus how much he and the others had given up to follow him, expecting the kind of answer Jesus gave: "You'll get back a hundred times what you've given up." But then Jesus had taken just a little gloss off their hopes by adding, "The last shall be first and the first last." While they were still muttering to one another, "What do you suppose he meant by *that*," Jesus went on to the story we've just considered. When Jesus finished, I can imagine one of the disciples turning to Peter and whispering, "That's a downer, isn't it?" and Peter answering, "He could have talked all day and skipped that one, as far as I'm concerned." Perhaps Peter added, "If I ever write a record of Jesus' teachings, I think I'll leave out that little story. No one will ever miss it, I'm sure."

Now tell the truth: You don't really like it, either, do you? Doesn't it strike you as unfair? How can one possibly contend that these people who worked only an hour should receive the same wages as those who put in a whole day, including the brutal heat of midday? What shall we say about a God who promises the same heaven to a self-centered scoundrel, saved on his deathbed, as to a Mother Teresa, who has spent a lifetime in the pursuit of holiness and in service to others?

The answer can be found in the late-afternoon dialogue between the landowner and the un-hired hands. He challenges them: Why have you been standing there all day, doing nothing? Why have you wasted your lives away, so to speak? In a world where there is work to be done, why have you been idle in the marketplace? The landowner wants a good reason from these idle persons if he is to venture them a place in his vineyard. Badly as he needs workers, he nevertheless isn't about to engage these people if their idleness is without explanation.

Their answer is poignant and almost beyond refutation: *Because no one has hired us.* They wanted to be employed. They were seeking employment. That's why they had been in the marketplace all day. But no one had hired them.

There is an experience deep in my memory which helps me understand these workers. I am blessed with many vivid memories of childhood, but none more vivid than a sunswept October afternoon in 1932 when I came bounding home from school, eager to tear off school clothes and put on playground stuff. But to my surprise, Dad was at home. This was unthinkable at three-thirty in the afternoon. Mother and two of my older sisters were standing with him. No one was seated; three were leaning against the kitchen sink and the other against a chair.

"Why are you home, Dad?"

Dad was generally slow to speak, but especially so at this moment, and Mother quickly filled the gap. "Daddy's lost his job."

Until then, I didn't know that good people could be unemployed. I thought only lazy people were without jobs, people who wouldn't apply themselves or who didn't deserve a job. This was the sort of ethic I had unconsciously imbibed while listening to adult conversations. But for the next eight or nine years I was to live in neighborhoods where many, from time to time, for shorter or longer periods, occupied themselves any way they could because "no one had hired them."

That's why I empathize with these un-hired hands and why, for me, the parable centers on them. If they are not the heroes, then they are, at least, the most sympathetic characters. Because I grew up during the Depression, I find the un-hired hands poignant. I know of few experiences that leave a human being more demoralized than to realize no one wants to hire you.

But no matter how poignant my memory of the Great Depression may be, there is something far more poignant. Eternally so. The response "because no one has hired us" represents, to me, a waiting world. It is a picture of the pathos of those millions of people who go through their lives with an almost unceasing emptiness, while they wait for someone to "hire" them.

I'm not talking about jobs and the world labor market, though that is in itself a serious enough problem. I speak rather of what we might call *having a purpose in living.* There are in our world ceaseless multitudes who want desperately to know that life amounts to something, that there is some purpose in their living, a reason to inhabit this planet.

Rudyard Kipling said that the Colonel's lady and Judy O'Grady are sisters under the skin. Certainly it is so in this matter. No economic class is exempt from the search for meaning, nor is any intellectual group. The hunger may at times be all the more intense among those who have attained some measure of success in their economic or intellectual pursuit, because in their achievement they have discovered that what they sought is not enough. As long as some goal is unreached—a certain amount of wealth, an educational landmark, a position of prominence—you can continue to tell yourself that if only you get "that," you'll be happy. But if you've got "that" and find you're still unhappy, how great, then, is that unhappiness.

Hardly anything is as pathetic as feeling unwanted. This is the ultimate tragedy of the soul wandering in loneliness on city streets or living obscurely in small-town isolation; or it is the kind of mental illness which causes a person to withdraw from society, usually because that person has become convinced that society has already withdrawn from him or her.

If it is tragic to feel that no person wants you, then think how profoundly tragic it is to feel that life itself doesn't want you. How dreadful to stand in life's marketplace all day long, while life doesn't hire you! Others rush by, apparently with an assignment and a purpose in living. But you stand waiting, wondering if ever life will say to you, "I have a place for you. There's a reason for you to be on this planet, and here it is."

Vast numbers of human beings stand in life's marketplace all day, all the days of their lives, and life doesn't seem to care. It passes them by. They wait in the morning, through high school and college, but no call comes. They wait through the heat and clamor of midday, but no call comes. Soon it is mid-afternoon, and still life hasn't shown any interest in them. Late in the day you ask, "How have you spent your life?" And they answer, "I've been waiting all my life in the marketplace, but no one has hired me."

To get an idea of the seriousness of this matter, consider how many people in our world seem always to be seeking an escape from life. Some do it with drugs, including alcohol, others with a kind of frantic running about, as if they hope somewhere to find their worth. Consider, too, how many take their own lives each year, and how many more think of it but can't quite bring themselves to do it.

G. A. Studdert-Kennedy, a vigorous, earthy man, was known for his poetry as well as for his preaching in London. In one of his sermons, he put his feelings into a poem:

> I must have God. This life's too dull without,
> Too dull for aught but suicide. What's Man
> To live for else? I'd murder someone just
> To see red blood. I'd drink myself blind drunk
> And see blue snakes, if I could not look up
> To see blue skies, and hear God speaking through
> The silence of the stars.

Then Studdert-Kennedy apologized for his violent language and confessed that his hearers might be "much more civilized" than he. "You, perhaps, would be content with more refined and decent drugs, modern novels, problem plays, scandal, bridge, mild gambling, and all the proper apparatus we clever people use to dull the pain of boredom and the emptiness of life." You might not consider murder, he added, but you would hurry to the newspaper to absorb the story of a murder there. Then he said, "I must have God, a God whom I can know, and love, and live for. I must find a meaning for life."[3]

This is the issue for those workers the landowner found late in the day. They had been waiting all day, but no one had hired them. Look on them with compassion, not resentment. And ponder, as you observe the daily pattern of life around you, how many people may be living with the "pain of boredom and the emptiness of life." Wonder, particularly, what is the significance of those multitudes of people who tell you they're "bored." Is their ailment more than a passing mood? Are they, perhaps, people who are standing in life's marketplace at noonday, waiting for life to hire them?

Virginia Law Shell recalls a time when she resented a woman who had lived all her days indifferent to God. It seemed as if this woman's life had enjoyed so many favors, including a marriage that eventually made her a wealthy woman. Shell considered, by contrast, how she had been widowed on the mission field when her missionary husband was murdered, and she was left with three children to educate and no resources with which to do so. "At times," she writes, "I felt resentful when I compared our two situations. Then I realized something. The Christian life is its own reward."[4]

It is, indeed. I believe in heaven, but if I did not, I would still opt with all my being for the Christian life. I want to have a grand reason for arising in the morning, to know the candle is worth the burning, to see a purpose in life beyond stoking the furnace of the body so that it can continue running for another day. My Christian faith gives such a sure, clear purpose. It immerses the quantity of life in quality.

I was fortunate—so magnificently fortunate!—to become a Christian when I was not quite eleven years old. I was hired early in the morning, at the beginning of life's day. So it is that I have been blessed through all my life with a sense of life's purpose, value, and beauty. How dare I, then, be bitter about those who have waited all day in the marketplace, if at the end of the journey they are blessed with an eternity as good as mine? Shall I envy those who have gone through life with no clear goal, battling their way through disillusionment, ennui, and despair, because life hasn't hired them?

To the contrary! When I stand before the Great Landowner as he passes out the silver pieces of eternity, I might well take mine and say, "Give part of this to that poor soul who didn't come to faith in Christ until he was sixty years old . . . and to that woman who became a believer only when she was dying. I've been employed all my days, have been blessed by a purpose, even by communion with God. Give them part of my reward, because they stood in the marketplace for so long, because no one hired them, while my life was filled with purpose."

But for now, let us look around the marketplace of life and see if, perhaps, we can lead some waiting there to a place of employment. Let us go to life's corner, in Christ's name, and say, "God wants to hire you! I speak as one of his hiring agents. Stand idle no longer. There is meaning to be had in life. Come, quickly, to the vineyard of God's will!"

CHAPTER 11

Moses and the Fig Tree

LUKE 13:6-9: Then he told this parable: "A man had a fig tree planted in his vineyard; and he came looking for fruit on it and found none. So he said to the gardener, 'See here! For three years I have come looking for fruit on this fig tree, and still I find none. Cut it down! Why should it be wasting the soil?' He replied, 'Sir, let it alone for one more year, until I dig around it and put manure on it. If it bears fruit next year, well and good; but if not, you can cut it down.'"

A great preacher in another generation said that whenever he felt he was losing his listeners, he used illustrations to take them out to the country. That was a sure bet for preachers and teachers until the late twentieth century, because almost every person in a typical congregation either lived on a farm, had lived on one, or was related to someone who did. As a result, they found illustrations from nature both interesting and understandable.

Jesus followed the same principle. By "taking people to the country" he not only sustained their interest but also explained issues that confused them. One day some people had a particularly troublesome question. They had heard of some Galileans whom Pilate had killed while they were in the very act of worship. I venture they were no more appalled by the harsh, bitter crime than they were by the fact that God would allow such a disaster to come upon the devout, and in a time of worship at that. So they raised the question that may well be as old as our human race: *why?* Why would God allow such a thing to happen? The Jews believed fiercely in the justice of God, so when disasters happened, they concluded that it was because a person or a nation was being punished for evil that had been done.

Jesus answered that these who had died were no worse than their fellows, then warned his listeners, "I tell you that if you do not turn from your sins, you will all die as they did."[1] He then proceeded to take them to the country, telling them a parable from a world with which they were all familiar. A man had a fig tree in his vineyard, but when he looked for figs, he found none. He reminded his gardener that for three years he had been looking for figs and had been disappointed each year. Now his mind was made up: "Cut it down! Why should it go on using up the soil?"[2]

It was a sound business decision. Not only was the fig tree unproductive, it was using up resources of nature and the time of laborers, which might otherwise be invested productively.

But the gardener appealed for "just one more year." He promised the owner that he would double his efforts to save the tree by digging around it and adding fertilizer. If this extra effort were unsuccessful, he would agree to let the tree be destroyed.

It seems likely the parable is meant to refer to Israel as a nation. They had failed to fulfill their calling and God's expectations, and now they were drawing near to judgment. The parable can also be applied effectively to each of us as individuals. God expects us to be fruitful, and if we are not, we are in danger. Charles Wesley put it in dramatic terms in one of the most familiar of his hymns:

> Help me to watch and pray, and on thyself rely,
> assured, if I my trust betray, I shall forever die.[3]

Because of the severity of the message, we're inclined to read this as a parable of judgment. But it has been pointed out that in truth the emphasis is on life. The gardener and the owner were both aiming for productivity; the goal was life, and death was seen only as the last alternative. It is a parable of another chance.

I'm fascinated by the gardener. He dares to talk back to the owner, to reason with him, and yes, even to argue with him. He speaks with proper respect, but he makes his case with all earnestness: Give the tree another chance. He reminds me of Moses.

Several times during his trying years of leading Israel, Moses contended with God on their behalf. The most notable instance was on the occasion when the people began worshiping a golden calf while Moses was on Mount Sinai receiving the Law. The book of Exodus (chapter 32) reports an astonishing dialogue between God and Moses. God told Moses to hurry down to the people because they had sinned and rejected the Lord. "I know how stubborn these people are," God said. "Now, don't try to stop me. I am angry with them, and I am going to destroy them. Then I will make you and your descendants into a great nation."

Dare a human being argue with God? Moses dared! First he reminded God that the Israelites were God's people, not his. They were the people God "rescued from Egypt with great might and power." If they were now destroyed, Moses argued, the Egyptians would find pleasure in the whole matter. "Stop being angry," Moses urged the Almighty. "Change your mind and do not bring this disaster on your people. Remember your servants Abraham, Isaac, and Jacob. Remember the solemn promise you made to them." And the writer of Exodus says that the Lord changed his mind.

But Moses was not finished. When he came to the camp and saw the enormity of the people's sin, he felt he must return to the mountain to make a new appeal on their behalf. His prayer is one of the most extraordinary prayers in all of the Bible: "Please forgive their sin; but if you won't, then remove my name from the book in which you have written the names of your people." God answered that he would decide who would and who would not have a place in his book; nevertheless, he answered Moses' prayer, and the children of Israel were spared.[4]

The gardener of the parable was like Moses. He dared to argue with the owner of the vineyard. Like Moses, he pleaded for patience, for the granting of another chance. Like Moses, he reasoned with the one in power. And like Moses, he won.

There is something very challenging about the story of Moses' defense of Israel and the implied message in this parable. Are both stories telling us that we human beings can change the mind of God? We're often told that the purpose of prayer is not to persuade God but to change us so that the purposes of God can be accomplished, and surely this is often what happens when we pray.

It seems to me that it's not a matter of changing the mind of God, but a matter of recognizing that we too often treat circumstances as if they were God. Perhaps this parable can teach us, among other things, that we often give up too easily, and that we assume too readily that because circumstances are difficult, God must have ordained that they be that way. We give divine status to things-as-they-are, thus increasing the power of the difficulties that confront us.

People too often dispose of the enigma of human tragedies with the sentence, "Well, it must have been God's will, or it wouldn't have happened." Not so! We live in a world of conflict, one in which darkness seeks constantly to assert itself over the divine light. Much of what happens in our world is *not* God's will. That's why the prayer our Lord gave us includes the petition, *"Thy will be done*, on earth as it is in heaven." When we pray for God's will to be accomplished, we are acknowledging that sometimes God's will is not done; more than that, we are acknowledging that it never will be done unless we pray—and labor—to bring it to pass.

It surely would have been easy for Moses to conclude that it was God's will for the fumbling slave nation to be destroyed. As far as he could tell, that's what God was saying to him! Yet he dared to reason with God, to say, "This isn't really your will, is it? It can't be, from what I know your nature to be."

Perhaps Moses and the gardener understood a hard fact about our universe: that a judgment always hangs somewhere over our human race and over us as individuals. In a sense, we are always in danger of destruction. Some of the perils change—the Black Plague terrified our ancestors, as AIDS does our generation—but others are as constant as our human race. War, for example, has always had us on the brink, so that even in times of relative peace we wonder how long it will be until the next crisis comes. And the smaller, more intimate crises pass on from generation to generation: our heartbreaks and uncertainties and nameless dreads. Through it all we fear that we are not using our lives as we should, nor as God expects us to.

So the cry comes down from one generation to the next: "There's no fruit on this tree! Cut it down!" God is not making the threat; rather, the threat is built into the very nature of things. We live in a universe basically moral, because God has made it so, and if we insist on being immoral, the universe will get its due. If we persist in hating in a universe that was made to operate on love, we can expect that it will at last cut us down.

Then comes a gardener who says, "Give it another year." At times the voice of the gardener comes to us with a secular accent, for the longing of our human race is deep and pervasive.

Holden Caulfield, that rather unlikely hero of *Catcher in the Rye*, is a bewildered teenager, an enigma to his parents, and a pain to his teachers. But when he visits his younger sister during the weekend of his questing and wandering, he gets to the heart of the matter. Loving his sister as he does, he's able to say to her what he cannot say to anyone else—perhaps what he could not have said even to himself. Sometimes the things we feel most deeply cannot be articulated until we're with someone who, knowing it or not, draws from us insights that, before, we couldn't put into words.

Holden tells his little sister that he knows what he'd like to do with his life: He'd like to be "a catcher in the rye." When his sister asks what he means, he reminds her of the song, "If a body meet a body coming through the rye."

> Anyway, I keep picturing all these little kids playing some game in this big field of rye and all. Thousands of little kids, and nobody's around—nobody big, I mean—except me. And I'm standing on the edge of some crazy cliff. What I have to do, I have to catch everybody if they start to go over the cliff—I mean if they're running and they don't look where they're going I have to come out from somewhere and *catch* them. That's all I'd do all day. I'd just be the catcher in the rye and all. I know it's crazy, but that's the only thing I'd really like to be.[5]

Holden had the right idea. He saw, no matter the crudeness of his teenage vision, that vast numbers of people in our world (not only "these little kids") are falling over life's cliffs; and he wanted, like the gardener of the parable, to do something to help.

Too many of us think we hear the voice of God in the situation of despair. That is, we assume that the despair is the end of the story, an expression of God's judgment. We see that the times are out of joint and the forces of evil are great. We recognize that there is corruption in politics, and that the tie between governments and the corporate world is sometimes powerfully entrenched. We wonder how anyone can confront a problem as huge as the cocaine empire and its legacy of "crack mothers." We know that millions are starving while their political leaders carry on in detached comfort, and we wonder how anything can possibly be done. We are all too ready to treat these admittedly monstrous circumstances as if they were God. We canonize the voice of despair and prepare to cut down the fig tree. We won't do the cutting ourselves, but we will acquiesce in the judgment.

Often the order to cut the tree comes from an institution, and it is a reasonable voice. William Booth was part of a denomination—the Methodist New Connexion in England—which had a heritage of concern for human need. Yet when he and his wife Catherine felt they were called to the great city slums of England, their denomination was not sympathetic. When Booth insisted on street preaching, the New Connexion dismissed him, apparently forgetting that their founder, John Wesley, had come to his own greatest ministry more than a century before in outdoor preaching. As one author has put it, Booth "shook the teeth of conventional Christianity."

Without a doubt, leaders in the Methodist New Connexion considered Booth out of the will of God. He was talking back to the system, raising questions that propriety said should not be mentioned. As abrupt in manner as he often was, Booth was an impatient gardener who not only appealed that the fig tree be given another year but also declared he would give it such a year whether anyone agreed to it or not.

Booth was a vigorous, challenging gardener, but sometimes the gardener may operate with a quiet, unswerving commitment. When Katharine Butler Hathaway arrived at Radcliffe College, she was "shy and countrified," and from an "unfashionable school." Far worse, her body was badly misshapen from her years of spinal tuberculosis. She had every reason to expect to be shut out of the most attractive elements of life at Radcliffe. But when she enrolled she was given Catharine Huntington as her "older sister." Miss Huntington was a senior who was "beautiful and distinguished and talented"—all the things the younger Katharine was not.

Above all, Miss Huntington had the talent "to discern in an obscure person something rare and important and to make other people see it too—above all, to make the person in question feel it and be it." Hathaway says she was "one of those rare persons, a gardener among human beings," the kind of person who could bring out the best in people the way others can bring out the best in plants.[6]

Sometimes the scene is wondrously confused, so that we argue with ourselves even as we seem to argue with the Great Owner.

Lancelot Andrewes, the seventeenth-century saint and scholar (and one of the principal translators of the King James Bible), wrote such a prayer in his *Private Devotions*. He pleaded with Christ to despise him not, making the case as Moses might, or as would the gardener of our parable:

> despise not the cost of Thy blood,
>   whom am called by Thy name;
>
> . . . .
>
> despise not Thine own holy things.[7]

In the despair he felt for his sins, Andrewes pleaded with God to spare his soul and being, but on what grounds? Above all, he pleaded on the grounds that he had been bought at the cost of Christ's death, had been "called by Thy name," so that he was now—whether he seemed it or not—one of "Thine own holy things."

Our world is crammed full of lost, or nearly lost, causes, difficult people, and dying institutions (including some that perhaps ought to die), all of which seem to be consigned to be cut down. Logic demands that it be so, either by official act or by benign neglect. Then along comes a gardener, a Moses, who talks back—to the government, to family, to encrusted institutionalism, and even to God. "Give it one more year," the gardener says. "I will dig around it and fertilize it, and let us see if perhaps there is, even yet, a crop to be had here."

There is audacity in the gardener's request. It is more respectful and measured than Moses' dramatic either-or request, but it is of the same quality and it springs from the same kind of heart. Specifically, it believes that we must not give in to the voice that says the cause is lost or the person is worthless.

But the audacity is honorable, because the gardener promises to work at the matter. If he were not willing to dig around it and to involve himself in the fertilization, his presumed interest in the tree and his talking back to the owner would be blasphemous. This is what separates the gardeners from the relatively large number who say, "Somebody ought to do something about that."

The gardener dares to believe in the character of God. Such gardeners are unwilling to acquiesce to circumstances or "fate" as if they were the voice of God—even when, as in Moses' case, it seems as if God himself favors destruction; for there is a profound confidence in the established character of God, regardless of what the present evidence might say. The gardener knows beyond doubt that God cares about the pain of his universe.

I honor these gardeners. They belong to the Royal Order of Moses. It's a noble company you and I might seek to join.

CHAPTER *12*

I Wish I Could Sell You More

MATTHEW 25:1-13: "Then the kingdom of heaven will be like this. Ten bridesmaids took their lamps and went to meet the bridegroom. Five of them were foolish, and five were wise. When the foolish took their lamps, they took no oil with them; but the wise took flasks of oil with their lamps. As the bridegroom was delayed, all of them became drowsy and slept. But at midnight there was a shout, 'Look! Here is the bridegroom! Come out to meet him.' Then all those bridesmaids got up and trimmed their lamps. The foolish said to the wise, 'Give us some of your oil, for our lamps are going out.' But the wise replied, 'No! there will not be enough for you and for us; you had better go to the dealers and buy some for yourselves.' And while they went to buy it, the bridegroom came, and those who were ready went with him into the wedding banquet; and the door was shut. Later the other bridesmaids came also, saying, 'Lord, lord, open to us.' But he replied, 'Truly I tell you, I do not know you.' Keep awake therefore, for you know neither the day nor the hour."

Early in my ministry I resolved that I would treat every wedding as if there had never been one before and would never be another. I felt I had to enter each wedding and its attendant counseling and rehearsal in such a spirit because of what the occasion meant to the bride and groom. Even though I might have several dozen weddings a year, I wanted to see each one as the only wedding in the world.

This wasn't as difficult as I expected. One has to be pretty cynical to resist the enthusiasm of people planning a wedding. And that's true not only of starry-eyed young people. One of the most joyous weddings of my memory was for a bride of 78 and a groom of 82. Weddings seem to capture all of us in their excitement.

But our attitude toward weddings can hardly be compared with that of the first-century world. Modern weddings have to compete with a hundred other celebrations and excitements, including sporting events, concerts, and television; but a first-century wedding was essentially the only diversion of the year, except for the stated religious holidays. Understandably, all else in a Palestinian village was put aside for a wedding. The bride, groom, and guests were excused from many of their religious duties, and even a rabbi might leave his study of the law in order to be part of the festivities.

One can imagine, then, how the crowd leaned forward when Jesus said one day, "Let me tell you about a wedding." He need say no more in order to have their full attention.

There were ten virgins, Jesus said, who went out with their lamps to meet the bridegroom. The listeners, familiar with the symbols of faith, recognized several things immediately. All of the young women had a proper invitation to the event, all were virgins (a way of describing their purity of character), and all had lamps, a symbol of light in their lives.

Five were wise (or "sensible," as J. B. Phillips' translation puts it), and five were foolish. What was the distinguishing mark? All ten had oil in their lamps (the lamps would have been quite meaningless otherwise), but the five wise women "took oil in jars along with their lamps."[1] They carried an extra supply, to be ready for whatever might develop.

As it turned out, the bridegroom was later than the five foolish women had expected. This requires an explanation, because our wedding procedures are so different from those of the ancient Middle Eastern world—and for that matter, from current practices in many Middle Eastern villages. We know exactly when a wedding will take place. The invitation announces that it will be "half past the hour." Although I recall very few weddings that started at precisely the time announced, one can be pretty sure that the beginning won't be more than five to seven minutes beyond the stated time. But in the more leisurely world to which Jesus was speaking, only the groom knew for sure when he would arrive. He chose not only the hour, but even the day, and it could conceivably stretch over a fortnight of expectation.

He was obligated, however, to send a messenger running ahead, shouting to the village, "The bridegroom is coming! The bridegroom is coming!"

We don't know how long the ten virgins had been waiting, but we know that it was long enough that they were sleeping when the cry came.

One shouldn't seek significance in every detail of a parable; ordinarily a single, main point is intended, and what we draw beyond that is likely to be by a stretch of imagination. There is, however, some significance in a secondary matter in this parable: Jesus didn't chide the virgins for sleeping. What other than sleep could have been expected when they didn't know whether the bridegroom was coming today, tomorrow, or early next week? Life can't be lived at a continuing fever pitch. We need time for relaxation, for play, for the routine matters (like sleep!) that constitute the daily run.

With the announcement of the bridegroom's coming, the virgins began hurriedly, and probably a bit frantically, to prepare themselves. It was then that the foolish five discovered their failing; their lamps were going out, and they had no extra supply of oil. They appealed to their more conservative friends, who answered, "No . . . there may not be enough for both us and you. Instead, go to those who sell oil and buy some for your- selves."[2]

So the young women ran pell-mell through the village streets, even though it was midnight, in order to get additional oil. Meanwhile, the bridegroom arrived, so when the five foolish virgins appeared, the door was shut. They pleaded for entrance, probably explaining they were part of the original company and that it was only by a small mistake that they were now outside. But the bridegroom was unyielding. "I don't know you," he said.

Jesus summed up the story with a moral, something he rarely did: "Therefore keep watch, because you do not know the day or the hour."

Because this parable appears in the collection of Jesus' teachings about the last days it seems likely that he was applying it especially to the time of his return. The lesson is clear: We don't know when that day may be, but we should be ready, and the secret of being ready is in having an adequate supply of oil—that is, the Spirit of God—in our lives.

It is also appropriate to apply the parable to the issue of death. Death, too, will be a meeting with the bridegroom, and we have no idea when it will be. Life expectancy charts are meaningful only until we try to apply them personally. Then we realize that it doesn't really matter that a person of thirty-five can expect to live forty-two more years. An accident tomorrow or a medical diagnosis next week can change all of that.

Millions of people were reminded of life's uncertainty quite dramatically one Sunday afternoon. A college basketball star leaped high in the air for one of sport's most exciting moments, the slam-dunk shot, ran back to mid-court while the crowd cheered and the television audience smiled in gratification, and then collapsed suddenly. He was dead within an hour or so from an undetected heart ailment. If such a trained, disciplined athlete has no guarantee of life, millions reasoned in the quiet of their souls, then surely neither do we. True; we never know when the bridegroom will come in the guise of death.

There are also less dramatic but more insistent showdowns of which we know neither the day nor the hour. As surely as the planets run their course, you and I will have such occasions. I'm speaking of those crises which intersect life at any number of points. Some are as life-shaking as the death of a loved one or the prospect of major surgery; others are as shattering as divorce or estrangement from a child or a parent. They come at all ages and junctures of life. If you have a good memory, you can recall a number of events from childhood and adolescence which put you at the far edge of fear. Perhaps many of those experiences can now be dismissed as childish, but that doesn't diminish the very real impact they made on your life at the time. Psalm 23 speaks of the "valley of the shadow of death." In truth, life has literally hundreds of such valleys, some of small scale and some lasting only days or hours, but valleys of death, nevertheless.

I can guarantee two things about such experiences: first, that they will come, as surely as you live. Large and small, permanent and passing, they will come. I speak this not because I'm pessimistic about life, for in truth I'm a full-fledged optimist, but because I have lived long enough to know that it is true. Second, when we come to such dark valleys, we need desperately to have some light. At such moments, we need a lamp that will see us through.

Usually when we look at this parable, we concentrate on the ten virgins. They're the heart of the story, of course. But I want to lead you into this parable from the back side. I want to introduce a person who isn't mentioned in the story but who is implied throughout. I'd even dare to say that he is the most important character in the story, though he never appears. In many of life's dramas, both off and on the stage, the fate of the lead characters is determined by some minor, supporting person. As I see it, that's the case in this story. A minor character makes all the difference. I'm speaking of the dealer of oil, that unknown merchant on some busy street who first provided the virgins with their oil and to whom the five foolish girls came running when they saw that their lamps were going out.

I imagine him on the day when the girls made their initial purchase. He asks how much oil they want, and they tell him. He pauses momentarily. "Why are you buying this oil?" He can tell by their manner that it is for more than routine purposes.

"A wedding. We're part of a wedding."

"In that case you'd better get more. You never know how long the bridegroom will keep the party waiting, you know. It never hurts to have something extra."

They think he's simply taking advantage of their excitement. After all, it's his business to sell as much oil as possible. Or maybe he's just a bit of a worry wart, a kind of calamity howler. "We can always come back for more if we need it," one answers airily. The seller of oil shakes his head. He's heard this kind of talk before.

I understand the seller of oil, because I belong to the same trade association. I've spent most of my life trying to persuade people to get more light in their lives. It's a good idea, generally speaking, because the light which is in Jesus Christ opens the door to a fullness of life that cannot be compared to any other way of living. But it is especially important for those occasions of crisis we inevitably encounter— those death valleys where we so need to have enough oil to find our way.

I wonder how the oil merchant felt when the girls came pounding on his door after midnight, desperate to buy more oil. Did he tell them what was on his mind? Did he grumble, "I warned you silly girls, remember?" Perhaps he was too kind, and perhaps they were too frantic to allow any moralizing. But after they left he must have said to himself, "I told them to buy more. I know what wedding delays are like, and how much a person needs a good supply. When will people learn? Can't they understand that they can never have too much oil?"

I know the feeling well. I've received so many of the desperate calls of those laboring in dark places, where oil is badly needed. I remember a family of long ago whose adult daughter was about to make a decision they thought—with reason—might destroy her. She was to be in our city for a weekend, and although she didn't know me, they thought that perhaps I could help by talking with her. I agreed to do so; as a pastor, I was anxious to help any way I could.

Unfortunately I was unsuccessful. A few weeks later the mother said to me, rather reproachfully, "I hoped you'd be able to do her more good." I wanted, defensively, to answer, "I'm sorry, but I can't do in thirty minutes what you neglected to do for thirty years." But I didn't say it. Maybe I should have. Perhaps I should have said, "You have to keep buying oil year after year, so that when the time of crisis comes, there's stock on hand."

I'm not suggesting that by going to church regularly and by maintaining a faithful devotional life a person wins brownie points with God. But I do know by experience that when we keep buying oil week after week and year after year, we are more likely to have oil on hand when the valley is dark. It is as simple as that.

I've become especially conscious of the difference between the wise and foolish virgins by visiting hospital patients on the night before their surgery. I have met those "foolish virgins" who have spent most of their time absorbed in trivia and want now to get a cram course in divinity to prepare them for the eerie, early-morning pre-surgery routines. As a pastor, I have always done my best, but I know so often that I am being asked to do the impossible. I'm not speaking of someone's salvation; the grace of God is a wondrous thing. But the courage for tomorrow—ah, that's a matter to be worked through over the long pull of life, through the constant purchase of oil.

In contrast, I've known those people who have had oil enough. "The doctor says I have a fifty-fifty chance. That's pretty good! Even Ted Williams couldn't bat .500. And if I don't make it, preacher, I'm ready. Mind you, I'm not anxious to go; I love this life too much for that. But I'm ready."

John Wesley said of the first generation of Methodists, "Our people die well." He was testifying that they had oil in their lamps sufficient for the final crisis. I expect he would have agreed that the final crisis is nothing other than any other crisis, writ large. Bereavement, sickness, divorce, betrayal by friends, disappointment with ourselves—in all of these dark valleys, we need oil to light up the way.

Finally, there's a bothersome exchange in this story. When the foolish virgins realize their lamps are going out, they ask their friends for some of their oil, and the friends reply that they can't give it to them because they might not then have enough for themselves. "Go to those who sell oil," they said, "and buy for yourselves."

The sensible five are not as harsh as they may seem. They're simply underlining a fact of life: No one can make it on another person's oil. We have to go to the marketplace and buy for ourselves. I've wished often that I could give my small share of faith to someone in distress, but it isn't possible. We can encourage another person to buy and perhaps we can even inspire, but there is a point at which a soul is at last on its own. We can't make it on our parents' supply of oil, or our spouse's, or that of our dearest friend. We have to go to God's market and buy for ourselves.

This is a tragic story, and we don't like tragedies. When it ends, the five foolish virgins are outside, looking in and listening. Inside a celebration is going on, with laughter, food, fun, and music; but they're outside, beating on the door.

Remember, however, how Jesus described them. He didn't say they were bad or unwelcome, because in truth they were virgins and they were supposed to be part of the grand celebration. He said they were *foolish*. There wasn't a reason in the world why they should have missed the party, except that they didn't take advantage of the opportunity that was surely theirs.

I keep thinking of my colleague, the seller of oil. I imagine how hard he tried to persuade them to buy more oil on their first visit. Perhaps afterward he felt, as I often do, that he could have done more. Maybe he could have pressured them, insisted, imposed his thinking on them.

On behalf of that long-ago seller of oil, I make my appeal. Buy enough oil for life's crises, including the ultimate one. It's a buyer's market, and the price is within your reach. In Jesus' name, buy *now*. Buy lots! You can never have too much.

NOTES

CHAPTER 1: *When the Good Samaritan Is Bad News*

1. Elizabeth Burns, *The Late Liz* (New York: Appleton-Century-Crofts, 1957), p. 189.
2. Deuteronomy 21:23, Galatians 3:13.
3. Isaiah 53:3.

CHAPTER 2: *God Called a Party, but Nobody Came*

1. Luke 15:10 (rsv).
2. Christopher Smart, "Jubilate Agno," in *A Burning and a Shining Light*, ed. David Lyle Jeffrey (Grand Rapids: William B. Eerdmans, 1987), p. 332.

CHAPTER 3: *The Timid Soul*

1. In the New Testament world, the talent was a measure of weight, approximately 75 pounds, and represented a monetary worth of six thousand drachmas. As we use the word, "talent" refers to a person's gifts or abilities, so the word often causes confusion for a modern reader—perhaps all the more so since we tend so often to translate our talents into their monetary value.
2. Matthew 25:30 (niv).
3. Paul L. Moore, *Seven Words of Men Around the Cross* (Nashville/New York: Abingdon Press, 1963), p. 25.
4. J. B. Phillips, *For This Day*, ed. Denis Duncan (Waco, Tex.: Word Books, 1974), pp. 163, 164.

CHAPTER 4: *The Seasons of the Soil*

1. Luke 24:11 (niv).
2. Isaiah 55:11.
3. Luke 14:26.
4. George MacDonald, *Diary of an Old Soul* (Minneapolis: Augsburg, 1975), p. 17.

5. Leslie Weatherhead, "Where Is This Risen Christ?" in *20 Centuries of Great Preaching*, ed. Clyde E. Fant, Jr., and William M. Pinson, Jr. (Waco, Tex.: Word Books, 1971), vol. 11, p. 138.

CHAPTER 5: *The Sad Story of the Embarrassed Farmers*

1. Romans 7:21 (kjv).
2. II Corinthians 11:14 (rsv).
3. "This Is My Father's World," Maltbie D. Babcock.

CHAPTER 6: *Love Always Wins . . . Sometimes*

1. Jeremiah 2:5 (rsv).
2. Hosea 11:3*b*, 4*a* (rsv).
3. Matthew 23:37.
4. Philip Yancey, "God, the Jilted Lover," *Christianity Today* (May 16, 1986), p. 72.

CHAPTER 7: *Why Doesn't God Like Religious People?*

1. Amos 5:21, 24.
2. Samuel Shoemaker, in a sermon preached at Calvary Church, Pittsburgh, Pa. (pamphlet, n.d.).
3. Quoted by J. I. Packer, *I Want to Be a Christian* (Wheaton, Ill.: Tyndale, 1977).
4. *Harvard Magazine* (July-August, 1990), p. 7.

CHAPTER 8: *Pardon My Insistence*

1. Vachel Lindsay, "General William Booth Enters into Heaven," in *Modern American Poetry*, Louis Untermeyer, ed. (New York: Harcourt, Brace and Co., 1919 [1942 ed.]), p. 263.
2. Helmut Thielicke, *The Waiting Father*, trans. John W. Doberstein (New York: Harper & Brothers, 1959), p. 185.
3. Ephesians 5:18 (gnb).
4. C. S. Lewis, *Surprised by Joy* (New York: Harcourt Brace and Co., 1955), p. 18.
5. Ibid., p. 170.
6. Ibid., p. 238.

CHAPTER 9: *The Prodigal Who Stayed at Home*

1. Luke 15:12*b* (niv).
2. Luke 15:2 (niv).
3. Sybil Canon, "The Question," *Guideposts* (June 1989), pp. 42-44.
4. *The Pulpit Commentary*, ed. H. D. M. Spence and J. S. Exell (New York: Anson D. F. Randolph & Co., n.d.), *St. Luke*, vol. 2, p. 49.

CHAPTER 10: *A Case for the Un-hired Hand*

1. Matthew 19:30 (niv).
2. Matthew 20:6*c*, 7 (niv).

3. G. A. Studdert-Kennedy, "The Word with God," in *The Word and the Work;* rprd. in *20 Centuries of Great Preaching* (Waco, Tex.: Word Books, 1971) vol. 9, p. 284.

4. Virginia Law Shell, "Our Want for Prosperity," *Good News* (January-February 1991), p. 36.

CHAPTER 11: *Moses and the Fig Tree*

1. Luke 13:5 (GNB).

2. Luke 13:7c (GNB).

3. Charles Wesley, "A Charge to Keep I Have.

4. All quotations from Exodus 32 are from the GNB.

5. J. D. Salinger, *The Catcher in the Rye* (Toronto/New York: Bantam Books, 1964 ed.), p. 173.

6. Katharine Butler Hathaway, *The Little Locksmith* (New York: Coward-McCann, 1942), pp. 178, 179.

7. Lancelot Andrewes, *The Private Devotions of Lancelot Andrewes,* trans. John Henry Newman (Nashville/New York: Abingdon-Cokesbury Press, 1950), pp. 8, 9.

CHAPTER 12: *I Wish I Could Sell You More*

1. Matthew 25:4 (NIV).

2. Matthew 25:9 (NIV).

Suggestions for Leading a Study of *Parables from the Back Side*

Welcome to a journey that explores the parables of Jesus from several unique angles. This leader's guide is intended to enhance your study and discussion of *Parables from the Back Side: Bible Stories with a Twist*.

As you begin exploring these parables, keep in mind that people learn in a variety of ways. Some people like to learn by analyzing information in a step-by-step process; others by visualizing information—creating a picture in their mind that represents the information that may or may not be in any order; others by thinking more abstractly. Some people may learn using a combination of these methods. People approach Bible study in different ways.

This leader's guide is written to help you look at the parables in a variety of ways, taking into account the different ways by which people learn. Some questions will ask that you think logically about the parable; others that you think emotionally; still others that you draw or paint or sculpt something to help gain insights into the parables.

Don't let this Bible study lead you. You lead it. Use the questions as you want. Don't feel the need to answer every question or complete every activity. If you find that one of the questions or activities leads you off into another discussion, feel free to pursue such a discussion as time and group interest allows and let the group journey as it will. At the same time, however, be careful that one person does not dominate the conversation. If this is a group study, the purpose is to get the entire group involved.

Leader's Guide sections. This leader's guide is broken down into various sections to help focus the discussion and to provide a guide for your study. You'll note that answers are not provided. Don't worry. Your role as leader is not to provide answers for every question. You are a learner too. Read the question (or write it on newsprint) and let the group respond. If the group is silent, offer your own thoughts as a starting point. Reading each chapter before the group meets and thinking about each question beforehand will make the task a lot easier.

If you'd like, pass this book along from one leader to another. Each chapter is written separately to let your group proceed at its own pace. While 40 minutes per chapter may be adequate for one group, others may want to take the whole hour. Still others may want to focus only on specific questions so that they can cover two chapters in an hour. Try one chapter with the group members and get a feel for how they would like to proceed.

Snapshot summary. A one-sentence summary of both the current and previous chapters (chapter 1 summarizes the book as a whole) offers a quick review for participants and provides continuity throughout the study.

Relationship questions. These questions are at the heart of the study and focus on our relationships with others, with God, and with the world. (The world encompasses the arenas of home, work, and church.) The parables themselves are about relationships. These three areas allow a group to focus on their particular interest. For example, a prayer group might focus on the questions that deal with God; a social action committee might want to focus on the world or others. Or a group might want to alternate using various sections from week to week. These three sections of questions are also intended to provide closure for each session—people can focus on one section that interests them particularly.

Activities. Each chapter provides a group activity as well as an activity that can be done at home individually. These are "doing" activities rather than just "thinking" activities. If your group is hesitant or embarrassed to participate, start out slowly and offer lots of encouragement. These are non-threatening exercises that may provide new learning experiences for many of the participants. Read the activity beforehand in case you need materials such as paper, pencils, or crayons.

Prayer. The prayer can be read by the leader, by a volunteer, or by the group to close each session. It can also be read in advance by the leader to help prepare for each session.

However you or the group decide to proceed with this journey, keep an open mind that leaves room for the Spirit to work. Try to relax and enjoy the experience as you discover anew the insights and challenges of the parables.

1. When the Good Samaritan Is Bad News

Snapshot summary of the book

This book looks at 12 different parables from the "back side." The "back side" means simply a different or fresh perspective in order to gain new insights about ourselves, our faith, and God.

Our relationship with others

1. What words come to mind when you hear the phrase *good Samaritan?*
2. Share a situation when you helped someone. In what ways was it rewarding or unrewarding?
3. Would you rather help others or receive help? Explain.
4. Think of a time when an "outsider" helped you. How did you feel?

Our relationship with God

1. Would you rather help God or receive help from God? Explain.
2. When has God surprised you with help from an unlikely source?
3. I avoid God's help in my hour of need by (check all that apply): ____ denying that I have a problem; ____ trying to "fix" the problem on my own; ____ discontinuing my prayers, Scripture reading, going to church, etc.; ____ promising to do better next time.

Our relationship with the world (work, home, family, church)

1. Jews avoided Samaritans and did not consider them neighbors. Whom do you avoid, or stay clear of, at work? In the church?
2. "Because someone is human and inhabits this planet with us, he or she is our neighbor" (Kalas, p. 13). In what ways do you agree or disagree with this statement?
3. Pick ONE word to summarize this parable. Explain your answer.

Activities

As a group: Rewrite this parable as though it happened today in your community. Use people, locations, and institutions that are familiar to you. Give everyone a chance to contribute. If your group has the interest and energy, act out your modern-day parable.

At home: Write a letter or postcard thanking someone who made you feel welcome in the past or who accepted you as an "insider."

Prayer: *Gracious God, you accept each of us as an insider. Help us to admit our need for help and to accept your love. Amen.*

2. God Called a Party, but Nobody Came

Snapshot summary

The parable of the good Samaritan in chapter 1 reminds us that God helps us in sometimes unlikely or unwanted ways. Chapter 2 explores the theme of celebration—or lack thereof—when sinners return home to God.

Our relationship with others

1. True or false: I like to spend time with sinners.
2. The worst sinners are those people who . . .
3. In the parable of the father and the two sons, how are you like the younger son? The older son? The father?
4. Share a time you wanted to celebrate something but had no one with whom you could celebrate.

Our relationship with God

1. Share a time you lost something and were thrilled to find it again. When has God been thrilled to find you?
2. I enjoy God's presence most . . .
3. Agree or disagree: God would like to have me at a party.

Our relationship with the world

1. What have been your happiest moments at church?
2. In what ways can you share your own joy with a friend? A spouse? A neighbor?
3. What kind of food summarizes this parable? Explain.

Activities

As a group: Have participants *first,* think of something they would like to celebrate, or for which they would like to thank God; *second,* choose a song that symbolizes that for which they are thankful; *third,* share their event and theme song with the group; *fourth,* sing together as a group each theme song.

At home: Watch a movie and try to answer these questions: Which character was the worst sinner? How would God celebrate with this person? How did people celebrate in the movie? What chances of celebration did people miss?

> **Prayer:** *Dear Lord, you have given me a special invitation to your party. Teach me to celebrate as I bask in your love. Amen.*

3. The Timid Soul

Snapshot summary

Chapter 2 explored the theme of celebration when sinners return home to God. Chapter 3 encourages us to trust in God so that we can discover the gifts and grace God has given us.

Our relationship with others

1. It is easy to trust God with my (check all that apply): _____ career; _____ relationships; _____ family concerns; _____ financial concerns; _____ issues of faith (e.g., eternal life).
2. Share why you agree or disagree with the following statement: "God gives all people the same opportunity."
3. Do you think the slave who invested one talent was timid? Why or why not?

Our relationship with God

1. When growing up I was taught to:
   a) fear God; b) see God as my friend
2. In what ways are you timid or fearful of God?
3. I can use the gifts God has given me in these ways . . .

Our relationship with the world

1. Can we be successful if we believe hard enough? Explain.
2. How does your church encourage others to use their talents and gifts?
3. What person has been most supportive to you and your dreams? Explain.

Activities

As a group: Have the group sit together in a circle and ask for a volunteer. Have everyone in the group share one positive affirmation or gift about this volunteer. Sentences can begin: "I think you'd be good at this because . . ." or "One thing I appreciate about you is . . ." Go on to the next person and do the same. Take turns, allowing each person to receive these affirmations from the entire group.

At home: Ask a spouse, child, friend, or parent what he or she sees as gifts that God has given you. Thank God for these gifts and think about ways to use these gifts on a daily basis.

> **Prayer:** *Dear God, many things in the world clamor for our attention. Help us to trust you and to be strong in your love. Amen.*

4. The Seasons of the Soil

Snapshot summary

Chapter 3 discussed ways to trust God with the gifts God has given us. Chapter 4 explores the seasons—times and ways—that we are open or not open to God's work in our lives.

Our relationship with others

1. Think of a person who has a rich faith life. What about this person's faith is most appealing to you?
2. When in your faith journey have you felt most alone? Explain.
3. In what ways do you agree or disagree with the following: God gives everybody the same chance to experience God's love.

Our relationship with God

1. I have seen God's hand in my life in the following ways . . .
2. Which of the following apply? God's involvement in my life:
   a) is ongoing.
   b) depends on how good I am.
   c) depends on my openness to God.
3. The thing that brings me closest to God is . . .
4. I find opportunities to discover God through: ____ prayer; ____ Bible reading; ____ discussions about faith; ____ other

Our relationship with the world

1. What was your image of God as a child?
2. What "weed" or thing distracts you most from God? Explain.
3. What opportunities do you offer at church to enrich people's faith?
4. In what ways can you make the "soil" or situation at home more fertile for faith?
5. In what silent ways can you live out your faith at work?

Activities

As a group: Pass out paper and crayons. Have members of the group draw their current relationship with God as a season in the year (spring, summer, fall, winter) and explain the drawing.

At home: Write a poem using free verse, rhyme, and so on, about a time when you were especially in tune to God's involvement in your life.

Prayer: *Master Sower, make my life a fertile place for your love.*

5. The Sad Story of the Embarrassed Farmers

Snapshot summary

Chapter 4 discussed the faith seasons in our life and our openness to God's work. This chapter reminds us that even though our world is full of weeds and wheat, good and evil, God is the Master Sower who can work powerfully in our lives.

Our relationship with others

1. Kalas writes that "rooting up and sorting out is a work for angels" (p. 44) rather than for sinful humans. In what ways do you agree or disagree?
2. Share an example of a person who was a "weed" that changed to "wheat."
3. With which of the following do you agree most?
   ____ There should be no hypocrites in church.
   ____ The church is a place for hypocrites.
   ____ Everyone who sins is a hypocrite.

Our relationship with God

1. What is the worst influence, or weed, that keeps people away from God? Explain.
2. Complete the following. People could get closer to God . . .
3. One way I feel that God is working in my life is . . .

Our relationship with the world

1. Which of the following forms of judgment are most pervasive at work? At church?
   ____ gossip   ____ judging people by outward appearance
   ____ rumors   ____ judging people before you know them
2. Share a time when you felt as though you were judged at a church for your clothing, cultural background, race, or other.
3. "Everyone has a right to enter the kingdom of heaven, but no one has a right to shut anyone else out" (p. 46). In what ways do you agree or disagree?

Activities

As a group: Read the following out loud to the group and discuss if the item is "wheat" or "weed" (whether it furthers God's work or hinders God's work in the world): ____ television; ____ requirement to tithe (give 10% of income); _____ music; _____ rules that keep people out; _____ wine; _____ special privileges for church members.

At home: Ask three people to answer this question: "The church would be less hypocritical if it . . ."

Prayer: *Lord, our life and our world belong to you. Help us find fitting ways to serve you and those around us. Amen.*

6. Love Always Wins . . . Sometimes

Snapshot summary

The last chapter showed how God works in our lives and in the world for good. Chapter 6 shows how God continues to risk his love for us, even though we do not deserve it.

Our relationship with others

1. Describe a time when love didn't win.
2. Do you think people can err on the side of being too generous? Why or why not?
3. In what ways do you think love is risky?
4. How have other people taken risks for you because they loved you?

Our relationship with God

1. Is God's love too easy or too difficult to receive? Explain.
2. How would you answer if God asked you, "Why haven't you responded to my love?"
3. Write down five ways that God has shown his love for you.
4. I hesitate to accept God's love in these ways . . .

Our relationship with the world

1. Explain why the following is either true or false: If people get the chance, they will take advantage of the love extended by others.
2. How do you risk your love at work? With those in your family?
3. Which of the following shows the risk of love?
   a) Asking for forgiveness.
   b) Forgiving someone else.
   c) Admitting your weakness to others.

Activities

As a group: Debate this statement in two groups: People choose a self-destructive life-style because they want to.

At home: Write down a way that you will take a risk with your love in the next week. Record the steps and actions you took in this venture of risky love.

> **Prayer:** God, you have risked everything to love me. Let me accept your love, and in turn, risk this love with others. Amen.

7. Why Doesn't God Like Religious People?

Snapshot summary

We discovered in chapter 6 that even though our love may at times be questionable, God takes the risk to keep loving us. In this chapter we see that the very things we do for the sake of religion can keep us away from God.

Our relationship with others

1. Share a time when you have wondered, Why me, Lord?
2. I am like the Pharisee when I (check all that apply): _____ read my Bible daily; _____ give 10% of my income to church; _____ pray regularly; _____ thank God for who I am.
3. Who would be the present-day tax collectors—people whom "religious folks" might despise?

Our relationship with God

1. "The Pharisee was using religion to hold God at a distance" (p. 64). How can religious ceremonies or practices keep us from God?
2. What things in the church draw you closer to God?
3. Do each of the following help you or hinder you from growing in your faith: music; money; religious paintings and relics; the liturgy? Explain.
4. What is the greatest demand God places on you as a believer?

Our relationship with the world

1. In what ways do you agree or disagree with the following: When dealing with others at work, home, or church, it is better to follow the rules than to follow our heart and feelings.
2. I try to avoid sin because: ___ of its social consequences; ___ I dislike sinning; ___ I don't want to hurt God; ___ I don't want to get caught.
3. How have you seen this parable occur at work or in the church?

Activities

As a group: Draw a stick person on a large sheet of paper. Above the person write the word *Pharisee*. Ask the group to list characteristics of a perfect Pharisee. Write their suggestions on the sheet of paper, discussing each one. *At home:* Every day for the next week tell God of three areas where you need God's help. Thank God for a love that will never let you go.

> **Prayer:** *Dear God, help me realize my need for you so that I might rejoice in the freedom your love allows. Amen.*

8. Pardon My Insistence

Snapshot summary

The last chapter explored how religion or religious practices could keep us away from God if we are not careful. Chapter 8 shows God's insistence about drawing us close, of inviting us to the great banquet feast to come.

Our relationship with others

1. Share a time when someone has enthusiastically shared his or her faith with you. How did you feel? How did you respond?
2. *Winsome* and *joy* are used to describe the attitude of a Christian who is sharing God's invitation. Should Christians always be happy? Why or why not?
3. Do you find it easy or difficult to invite people to a party? Explain.

Our relationship with God

1. Check those excuses below that you use to refuse God's invitation of love: ____ I don't have time; ____ I'm waiting for a better time; ____ I'm not good enough; ____ I'm waiting until I understand God better.
2. Share a time when your faith made you feel joyful.
3. How do you experience God's banquet feast today?
4. When has God been persistent in your own life?

Our relationship with the world

1. How does your church associate with people who live on the edges of life?
2. How might your church be more inviting to others in extending God's invitation of salvation?
3. Check all those responses that apply. *Insistence* means: ____ witnessing to others; ____ reminding ourselves of God's great love for us; ____ telling others, even those who don't want to hear, of God's invitation; ____ other.

Activities

As a group: In groups of two or three, rewrite this parable as though it took place today. Ask each group to read its story aloud. What was similar or different about these modern-day parables?

At home: Make an invitation from God inviting you to an event of your choice. Color or paint the invitation. Include a positive response to the invitation.

> **Prayer:** *Gracious Lord, remind us daily of your open invitation for your feast prepared for us. Help us joyfully share this invitation with others. Amen.*

9. The Prodigal Who Stayed at Home

Snapshot summary

Chapter 8 shared how God's insistent love invites us to God's joyful feast. In this chapter we see how we, like the older brother, may take God's love for granted or be jealous of God's great love for others.

Our relationship with others

1. Share a time when you felt like the older brother, when someone received something he or she didn't deserve.
2. Which of the following statements do you think would be said by the older brother: (a) "That person doesn't deserve it"; (b) "I've been good all my life"; (c) "Life isn't fair"; (d) "God isn't fair"; (e) "Strangers are welcome here."
3. The person I find most difficult to love is . . .

Our relationship with God

1. List 10 things in your life for which you can thank God.
2. How have you taken God's love for granted?
3. When has God's love felt most real to you?

Our relationship with the world

1. "The older brother had never really discovered the joys of home" (p. 81). What does this mean for you in your own home situation?
2. What things do you take for granted about your church? Your work?
3. How could your church be more accepting of those in your community?
4. If you were to visit your church as a guest, would you feel welcome or unwelcome? Explain.

Activities

As a group: Ask for volunteers to play the roles of the father and the older son. Pretend that the rest of the group are acting as newspaper reporters who have arrived just as the father is talking to his disgruntled son. Interview these two people about the situation.

At home: Think of a time in your own life when you felt like the older brother. On a sheet of paper, write down your thoughts, feelings, and reasons for being hurt. If the situation is still unresolved, ask God's guidance in working in the midst of hurt feelings to resolve the situation. Toss the paper as you give the situation over to God.

Prayer: *Our Father in heaven, hallowed be thy name. Thank you for your gracious, welcoming, and abiding love, now and forever. Amen.*

10. A Case for the Un-hired Hand

Snapshot summary

Chapter 9 showed us how God welcomes us home despite the fact that we may take God's love for granted. Chapter 10 points out God's grace for all people, no matter when we discover God's love for us.

Our relationship with others

1. Share three things outside the church that add meaning to your life.
2. To me, the "pain and boredom and the emptiness of life" (p. 91) means . . .
3. Think of the first time you experienced God's love. Share this experience with another person.

Our relationship with God

1. Do you think it is unfair that people receive the same gift of eternal life, whether they are believers for a lifetime or become believers on their deathbed? Why or why not?
2. What are the advantages of knowing God's grace early in life? (Think of forgiveness, the sacraments, and so on.)
3. Share a time when you felt like an un-hired hand, waiting for God to demonstrate God's love for you.
4. God shows me grace every day by: _____ giving me food and shelter; _____ giving me decent health; _____ accepting me freely despite my sin; _____ providing others in my life who care for me and love me.

Our relationship with the world

1. Share a time when you felt particularly welcome at work, home, or in the church.
2. Pretend that you are an employer in your community looking for hired hands. Where would be the marketplace? Who would be the un-hired hands?
3. Discuss G. A. Studdert-Kennedy's poem on page 91. What speaks to you?
4. List three ways you can mirror God's grace at work, at church, and at home.

Activities

As a group: Write a want-ad for your church describing the kind of people you'd like as members. Examine your finished ad. In what ways does it welcome people at all stages of life? How does it reflect God's grace?

At home: Think about your favorite job. Draw or paint the things that made it enjoyable and meaningful. Thank God for the ways he can work anew in your life with his grace.

Prayer: *Gracious Lord, you come to us in the morning, in the noonday, and in the evening. Help us receive your undeserved grace. Amen.*

11. Moses and the Fig Tree

Snapshot summary

The last chapter focused on God's grace as it comes to us at all times in our lives. This chapter reminds us that God is for life and can work in and with us to bring life to others.

Our relationship with others

1. Share a time when you got another chance.
2. What things in the world threaten you on a daily basis (e.g., events, people, other)?
3. What person, institution, or cause could benefit from your care? Explain your answer and how you would carry out your program.

Our relationship with God

1. How is God's forgiveness like "another chance"?
2. Is it appropriate for humans to argue with God? Why or why not?
3. Do you think everything that happens is because of God's will? Explain.
4. In what ways has God nurtured and cared for you, either directly or through another person?

Our relationship with the world

1. In which of the following ways are you evaluated at work? At home? At church? (a) By the amount of work I accomplish; (b) By my good intentions; (c) By what I do for others.
2. In what ways does your church focus on judgment? On life?
3. Think of three ways you can bring out the best in others at work and home.

Activities

As a group: Have the group cut out events or words from a daily newspaper that give cause for despair (e.g., violence, fear, hunger). Next, find ways that God can work in the world to bring comfort, hope, or resolution to this despair.

At home: Write down on a sheet of paper 6 to 12 people important to you in your circle of friends, family, work colleagues. How have you enriched their lives? How can God use you to enrich their lives?

Prayer: *Living God, your will is that all people might have life in you. Increase this life in us so that we can nurture those around us. Amen.*

12. I Wish I Could Sell You More

Snapshot summary

Chapter 11 focused on God's grace for us and through us as we attempt to live our lives for others. This chapter deals with God's readiness to give us grace and love to prepare us for the unpredictable events of this world.

Our relationship with others

1. In general, do you feel that you are prepared or unprepared for most situations in life? Explain.
2. Describe a time when you were caught unawares and missed an opportunity.
3. Think of a "dark time" in your life. Was there a light that pulled you through? If so, what was it?

Our relationship with God

1. What do you think it means to be prepared for God?
2. Share a time when God worked in your midst to bring healing out of a painful situation.
3. In which of the following ways do you think God works? Share experiences, when possible, that support your answer. (a) through prayer; (b) through others; (c) through crisis; (d) through the church; (e) through study and Bible reading.
4. What preparations for death would you like to make today?

Our relationship with the world

1. What are the different sources of light in your life?
2. When you read the following quote, what comes to mind? "We can't make it on our parents' supply of oil, or our spouse's, or that of our dearest friend" (p. 107).
3. In what ways did your parents, relatives, or friends, help prepare you or train you for faith?
4. How can you help prepare or train others for a relationship with God at home, work, or at church?

Activities

As a group: Using a piece of tinfoil (about 12" x 24"), sculpt a time of crisis in your life. Create moods, feelings, people, or objects with your foil. If you feel comfortable doing so, explain your creation to the rest of the group.

At home: Read Psalm 23 once a day for a week. Focus on the words, sentences, and images as a way for God to work in your life.

> **Prayer:** O Lord, you are constantly ready to give us that which provides life. Help us prepare our days by relying on your mercy, forgiveness, and saving love. Amen.